SIX SCILLY
SWIMMERS

SIX SCILLY SWIMMERS

ATTEMPTING A WORLD FIRST

MARK RANSOM

Published by Mark Ransom
Edited by Mark Ransom and Cherie Ransom

Six Scilly Swimmers logo designed by Oliver Hilton
Printed by Kindle Direct Publishing

Photo credits: Six Scilly Swimmers, Frederick Buckingham, Kate Robarts, Steve Robarts, Veronika
Mikyskova, Neil Brinkworth, Rich Devey, Joel Whittingham, Steven Andrew
Photos edited by Alexandra Cave

ISBN: 9798322622239

This book is dedicated to:

Philip Jones 5th March 1949–12th June 2021
(Sam's dad)

Clara (Clair) Ransom 28th January 1929–25th April 2023
(my mum)

Monika Baylis 5th January 1949–3rd October 2023
(my mother-in-law)

Gina Cuddy 30th May 1972–22nd February 2024
(my dear friend)

Christine Taylor 11th June 1953–29th May 2024
(my sister)

and

David Wilkie MBE 8th March 1954–22nd May 2024

ACKNOWLEDGEMENTS

Cherie, Scott, Sean and Phoebe. My mum. Danielle Irvine, Veronika Mikyskova, Stu Fox, Maggie Kidd, Kerrie Bailey, Beth French, Vicky Middlemast, Oliver Hilton from Precision, Dr Unsworth, Seamus Bennett, Louise Stratford, Steven Andrew, Amber Baylis, Joan Bennett, Amanda Bell, Cheryl Rolfe, Mark Gordon and Owen.

Six Scilly Swimmers:
Sam Jones, Richard Pearce, Mark Ranson, Darren 'George' Maguire, Megan Sanders, Cathy Freeman-Brown.

Official observers:
Kate Robarts and Neil Brinkworth.

Our boat crew:
Pilot Mark Johns, Fred Buckimgham, Andy Bennetts.

Team West Suffolk:
Ria Delves, Richard Pearce, Mark Ransom, Darren 'George' Maguire, Tia Whittingham, Cathy Freeman-Brown.

Team East Suffolk:
Carl Friar, Simon Pryke, Joseph Foot, Samantha Nicholls, Mark Barham.

A huge thank you to everyone who has given advice and shown their support and encouragement for our relay swim. Also to all those who have sponsored us and helped raise a huge amount for the RNLI.

INTRODUCTION

Swimming across the English Channel, both as a solo swimmer and as part of a relay, was the subject of my first book. Never wanting to stay in my comfort zone for too long it was time to up the game a little. This was largely as a result of Cathy's gentle and persistent encouragement of me, to keep our swimming adventure going.

This book carries straight on from where my first one finished and gives my personal account of what happened next. Believe me, what happened next was like nothing any of us expected or even hoped for. It details how plans sometimes have to change, and obstacles be overcome. As is always the nature of this sport, we also had the constant unease that our swim would not even start, especially as there was a storm heading across the Atlantic towards us in the days leading up to our planned swim window.

It certainly was not an easy ride by any stretch of the imagination. There was a birth, a death, a respiratory arrest, a broken leg, two of the team undergoing surgery, a shoulder cuff injury and of course lockdown – preparation for this swim could certainly have gone a lot better for the team!

Our swim to the Isles of Scilly was like a journey into the unknown for all of us, but that's what made it exciting. We didn't know quite what to expect and we wouldn't find out what it would actually be like until the day itself. The Atlantic Ocean certainly proved to be quite a different swimming experience to the English

Channel and we all embraced it, and maybe even enjoyed it at times.

Everyone in the team had their own personal challenges to get through on their journey to us finally coming together on the day as one unit and all performing collectively to achieve our goal. This goal was to become the very first relay team to swim from mainland Britain to the Isles of Scilly under English Channel swimming rules. Although this was a very big task to undertake, I have to admit that when I originally researched this swim, I was very surprised that no relay team had ever completed it before. Someone had to be the first relay and so why shouldn't it be us?

Each member of this team will have their own personal account of their journey through this wonderful adventure of ours. This is my account, from the viewpoint of my personal experience, and I have kept it as factually accurate as I possibly can. I do this through meticulous note taking and record keeping which some may consider a bit nerdy. But when it comes to writing an account of something, these notes are like gold dust. I can quote things that some of my teammates have said because I have noted it down. A couple of years later they have no recollection of saying these words, but I have that record. I have also used the reports of our official observers and one of our boat crew (with their permission), as well as looking at old Facebook posts and messages between our team to research this book. This is my story of our team taking on a huge challenge and I hope you enjoy it.

ONE

TRIUMPH

The emotions inside me had reached their full intensity as I dived into the refreshing cool sea knowing I had only a short sprint to the shore to complete our English Channel relay swim. I loved every second of that swim towards the French coast. As I glided through the water, I was simply buzzing with excitement at what our team was about to accomplish. Only about three minutes later I felt my hand touch the soft sand beneath the water and I knew we had made it. I stood up with a huge grin on my face and as I waded through the shallow water and out onto the warm sandy beach on the south side of Wissant, I was greeted by a family enjoying a day out and I also heard clapping and cheering from people up on the clifftop. It was the most wonderful and unexpected reception we were receiving. I knew my teammates were following closely behind me and I couldn't wait for them to join me on the shore to celebrate. The exhilaration I was experiencing was almost overwhelming.

A minute or so later the rest of the team emerged from the water looking triumphant, and as they walked up the golden sand towards me, there were big smiles and outstretched arms for a congratulatory hug. Next, I had the honor of popping the cork on the bottle of Prosecco that had been brought ashore along with plastic 'glasses' so we could have a celebratory drink. Photos were taken by the welcoming family and Tia also filmed the moment on her phone, but it all ended far too quickly, and we soon found ourselves once again back in the sea and swimming out towards our escort boat *Suva*, stopping briefly to pose for a photo in the water, before climbing back on board.

It was a beautiful sunny day in mid-July and the landing in France couldn't have been more perfect. This was a far cry from the rough conditions we had started this challenge in the previous night. Conditions that were so bad, we had been advised not to even begin the swim. But we started it anyway and battled against the odds. We had soldiered on through those awful and hellish first few hours, being battered by fierce waves in the darkness, causing us to feel disorientated and desperate for our individual hour stints to be over. While swimming in these conditions our adrenaline was at an all-time high as our survival instincts kicked in. Simply breathing in those vicious waves in the dark was so difficult and we probably swallowed more sea water than we ever imagined possible.

Despite all of this, we conquered the conditions and could now just relax and chill out on the top deck of our escort boat *Suva* and bask in our glory. However, there was also a degree of sadness in our hearts as our friends on Team East Suffolk, who were our 'competitors', had sadly been forced to pull out of the challenge during the night. Ideally, both teams would have been celebrating their successes together, but this was sadly not the case.

As we made our way back to England, the celebratory drinks of Prosecco had now turned to swigging from cans of beer. Not very glamourous I know, but then the whole business of English Channel swimming is never a very glamourous affair. I shared a bag of Doritos and a jar of hot salsa dip with Ria while we all relayed our experiences of the swim and generally took the piss out of each other. The recollections of me accidentally straddling a rope while jumping in for my second swim appeared to amuse them greatly. Although I was still feeling the pain from this error of judgement, I too found it hilarious and showed them with pride the huge bruise I now had in my groin. I was just very grateful that this incident hadn't resulted in a far worse injury had the rope struck me an inch to the left and the swim having to be aborted.

Sam came up on deck for a chat with us. Sam was one of the boat crew but also a close friend of mine. We had both swum the English Channel solo in 2008 and had also run a couple of marathons together. Sam had also been the person to encourage me to organize this swim in the first place and I was very grateful that she had done that, otherwise this moment may never have happened.

Team West Suffolk. From left: Ria Delves, Richard Pearce, Cathy Freeman-Brown, George Maguire, Tia Whittingham, Mark Ransom.

As *Suva* gently bobbed its way back to England, eventually the exhaustion and lack of sleep finally began to take its victims. I think Tia was the first to fall into a state of slumber, closely followed by Ria; in fact, we didn't quite finish our Doritos before she was gone. Cathy, George and I were still quite lively and had the delight of watching Richard trying to fight off the sleep, and I must admit he did put up a good fight. What we found most amusing was that the can of beer in his hand kept slipping sideways as he nodded off, and just before spilling it and soaking Tia, who was fast asleep next to him, he would jolt back to life as though he was still an active participant in our conversation. He would look at us with eyes wide open and an expression on his face that was certainly an attempt to convince us that he actually knew what was still going on. Obviously, he hadn't got a clue what we were talking about and was clearly no longer an active member of any conversation that was still taking place. It wasn't long at all before Richard joined the other two in the land of Nod and quite remarkably kept his can of beer upright. Now that's survival instinct if ever I saw it.

I'm not quite sure exactly when Cathy came out with it, but I'm pretty certain not everyone was awake to hear it. "So, when are we going to swim the North Channel?" she casually enquired while looking me directly in the eye.

I believe I let out a nervous laugh at this point before giving my simple reply. "Please can we at least get back to England before we discuss our next swim?"

I've said it before, Cathy is just simply too hardcore for her own good. I was well aware that the North Channel was maybe the next logical challenge for our team but I didn't want to discuss it right then. Maybe Cathy thought she would catch us while we were on a high and so we would obviously agree to anything. I somehow managed to change the subject and diverted the conversation back to celebrating our English Channel success, and before long, we were just chilling out to some music and casual conversation.

Once back in Dover we made our way to our hotel rooms for a short power nap before heading out for food and a proper celebratory drink in the famous White Horse pub. Landlord Stu Fox was delighted to hear of our success and we all proudly signed the English Channel relay swim book, which had been presented to The White Horse by the Channel Swimming & Piloting Federation.

Cathy and I on the way back from France.

The evening ended far too quickly for my liking, but we were all exhausted and in desperate need of some proper sleep. Back at the hotel I bid the others goodnight and then went for a walk along the promenade on my own.

I knew it was not quite time for me to sleep yet as I still had so much stuff to process in my head. It was a clear sky, and I noticed the stars winking at me, as I looked out over the dark, still water of the English Channel and felt the gentle warm breeze of a summer night against my face. The feeling was wonderful.

I needed this quiet time to reflect not only on what we had just achieved during the last day, but also on everything that had happened over the previous couple of years since I first started to organize this whole event. It hadn't been an easy journey at all and with Team East having to pull out during their swim, it certainly wasn't the ideal outcome. However, I had some amazing memories of this adventure with the rest of our team and also with our training and socializing with Team East, and I felt really sad and empty that it was now all over. It felt like I had come to an abrupt end of a chapter of a book, but the next chapter had not yet been written, and so I didn't know what would happen next. Maybe it would never be written? Maybe this was the end of all these adventurous swimming endeavours? My thoughts were becoming rather negative at a time when they should have been filled with joy. No longer would we be meeting up for our lovely evening swims in Felixstowe. There would be no more planning, no more team building, no more nervous anticipation. It appeared that there was just a huge empty void ahead of me and it was a depressing thought. I continued staring out to sea and looking for some comfort or even inspiration.

Then suddenly Cathy's voice popped into my head, "So, when are we going to swim the North Channel?"

At first this made me chuckle to myself because it reminded me of Cathy's hardcore personality, and how I had managed to divert the conversation away from this subject on the way back to England, because I simply wasn't ready for that discussion at the time. But then suddenly at that moment I felt really glad that Cathy had made that comment to me on the boat ride back to Dover. As a smile formed on my face, my gaze moved up towards the night sky filled with twinkling stars and a warm and comforting feeling established itself within me as it suddenly became very apparent that this swimming adventure was far from over.

TWO

FROM NORTH TO SOUTH

A week later Richard, George and I headed over to Felixstowe to meet up with Carl and Simon from Team East Suffolk. After a quick obligatory dip in the sea, we all sat down over a pint to discuss the whole experience of our English Channel swim. Richard, George and I really did feel for them and wished they could have had a successful crossing to France. Fortunately, Simon had previously been a part of a successful relay Channel swim, but for the rest of the team it was their first attempt and so this was clearly a huge disappointment for them. Carl vowed to return at some point as he had unfinished business with the English Channel, and I loved this attitude.

Following this evening in Felixstowe we continued to bask in our glory and promote our achievement on social media to raise more money for our two charities. We put a video together and I also wrote about the whole experience of our East vs West Channel Swim Challenge. This formed the last section of my English Channel swim book, which I published the following year.

With all the excitement of our successful swim followed by everyone returning to their 'normal' lives, there had been no more mention of any proposed North Channel attempt. As well as this, all swimming for me completely ceased. This was very similar to the experience I had following my solo swim back in 2008. It wasn't intentional, but I just didn't have any inclination or motivation to get back in the sea or the pool and swim. Maybe following a period of intense training, which resulted in my goal being achieved, I just needed to take a step back and recover fully. After all, this whole relay challenge had been one hell of a roller-coaster ride for me, physically, mentally and emotionally.

A further distraction for me personally were the troubles I was having at work. I had unfortunately witnessed a very serious incident in my job as a paramedic, which involved negligence by a manager and the subsequent death of a member of the public. Witnessing such a thing is stressful enough in the first place but then when I reported it, things took a turn for the worse like you would not believe. I experienced first-hand what it was like to be an NHS whistle-blower and the corruption and revenge that is brought down upon you by a management team that are desperate to sweep an incident under the carpet and pretend it never happened. The bullying and false allegations against me began and management all closed ranks and made my work life impossible. The impact on my mental health was devastating and the fact that they knew of my mental health issues, having previously been diagnosed twice with post-traumatic stress disorder (PTSD) in the line of duty, convinced me that they were trying to push me over the edge in the hope I would take my own life, like several other paramedics had unfortunately done around that time, and irradicate the whole problem for them. I know that sounds very extreme, but unless you have experienced it yourself, you cannot even begin to imagine the sheer depths that some NHS managers will go to if you dare cross their path. There is a reason that the NHS is totally broken right now and that is certainly not down to the very hard-working and dedicated staff. I personally believe it is predominately down to corrupt management, and I give this opinion from personal experience and having listened to so many other people who have told me similar stories of their own experiences. Eventually I could take no more and had no choice but to resign from the job I loved and had been doing for nineteen years. Attempts to take the matter further fell on deaf ears and everyone would automatically take the side of the Trust. I soon realized why I had heard so many nightmare tales from other whistle-blowers. I had hit rock bottom, was out of work and could see no future for me at all.

Eventually I managed to get a job as a carer in a nursing home and found it much more rewarding than I ever imagined. Despite being on a fraction of the wage I was used to, I loved what I was doing and knew I was making a real difference to other people's lives. Gradually I started to feel more like a valued member of society again, and with the help of medication and the support of others, I somehow managed to claw my way out of my deep depression and back to some kind of normality.

I was now working with some incredible people with hearts of gold. One in particular took me under her wing and taught me so much that I thought I already knew, but clearly didn't. Her name was Danielle, and we had such a great working relationship. The nurses recognized this and would always try to put us together on shift because they knew we were such a great team, and things would run smoothly and without any drama. Danielle was an honest and hard-working person who always tried to make the best of a bad situation and I really admired her for that. She also had a wicked sense of humour and sometimes her piss-taking was legendary! Working with Danielle didn't feel like work at all; I was simply spending the day with a wonderful friend.

Eventually, the time came when my paramedic registration was due for renewal, and I had to make that very important decision whether I remained as a carer or took the big step to try to return to work as a paramedic. I was terrified at the thought of going back to front-line work as I had lost so much confidence due to the way

I had been treated by the NHS Trust I had worked for. I also knew this could only be done in the private sector as I had certainly burned a thousand bridges with the old Trust I was employed by and there would be no going back for me.

I did look at other options for work as a paramedic, but they all wanted someone who had been working on front-line within the last year. Despite almost two decades of working front-line as a paramedic, they wouldn't accept my experience if it wasn't recent. One company said they really wanted to recruit me and asked that I just do the required six months front-line work and then get back to them. So, I managed to get a full-time job with a private ambulance company that provided work for East Midlands Ambulance Service (EMAS). This meant I was once again on a front-line ambulance and still attending to NHS 999 emergency calls. The job I had done and loved for many years.

On my first day back, I was nervous beyond belief, but somehow, I managed to get through it and was actually proud of myself that I had done a good job. However, it was not easy for me, and I just kept telling myself that it was only for six months and then I could get a job in the safety of an office or call centre.

Six months passed, and I was still struggling a bit but decided to give it a bit longer. I wasn't enjoying my work anything like I used to, but something made me stay for now. I told some of my colleagues that I probably wouldn't be staying that much longer as I had done my time on front-line and needed to move on.

Then one day, not long before Christmas, I had a shift with a new member of staff called Veronika who had only just started front-line work. I had heard that Veronika had joined our company, but I was yet to meet her. We first met at the start of our shift and after a quick introduction we were soon on the way to our first call and so we didn't have much time at all to try and get to know each other. Veronika told me she had done her training with St John's Ambulance, and I didn't know what this would have involved or how good this training would have been. However, as the day went on, and we spoke more, I realized that Veronika was a very capable Emergency Care Assistant and so I encouraged her to push herself that little bit further out of her comfort zone. After the shift Veronika thanked me for allowing her to get so involved as she had not been given those opportunities by anyone else.

I really enjoyed my shift with Veronika and was looking forward to my next one with her which was exactly a month later. We had another great shift together and then a third one. Until this point, I had lost all my enthusiasm for working on a front-line ambulance and was seriously considering that I should leave and contact the company that wanted to recruit me now that I had my six months, recent front-line experience. Then something happened that I was not expecting. Veronika asked if I would be her full-time crew mate and mentor her. By now I was self-employed and so I could choose when I worked and who I worked with. I was very flattered that Veronika had asked me to be her mentor.

Veronika and I got on extremely well and I could see great potential in her, and so I agreed to be her mentor. This was a huge turning point for me. Suddenly, I had some real purpose to staying on front-line duties as I had a very keen newbie who wanted to learn from my experience, and she really didn't disappoint. Bear in mind that English was Veronika's second language as she was from the Czech Republic. She had come to England for a holiday several years previously and decided to stay. At this point she spoke no English at all and struggled her way through various jobs while teaching herself to speak our language. She was a very determined young lady, and this became very evident when I worked with her. Veronika's work ethic was like nothing I had ever seen, and she also learned so quickly. It was very rare for me to have to explain something to her more than once. In all the years I had been mentoring students, I had never met anyone quite as remarkable as Veronika. Within six months she had learned so much that she was giving advice to technicians when she worked with them (they were a higher grade). Veronika also had an amazing sense of humour which often reminded me of Danielle. They could both be quite cruel at times, but all in good fun. Veronika would often refer to me as her retro paramedic because of the years I had done on the road. I was always having to correct her that the word was 'experienced' not 'retro'!

I am a true believer that everything happens for a reason and that people come into our lives for a reason. Danielle had helped to pick me up from a very dark place and showed me a reason for continuing and how to actually enjoy work again. Although I was helping Veronika to progress to eventually becoming a paramedic, in return she had given me a new zest for the job I had loved for so many years but feared was coming to an end. Both Danielle and Veronika are the reason I am where I am today. At the time of writing this, I am now enjoying my front-line work as a paramedic more than I have ever done in the past.

Danielle and I on a night out with friends.

Veronika and I enjoying some time out from work on the London Eye.

After the meeting in Felixstowe with Richard, George, Carl and Simon, an incredible eleven months had gone by without me swimming at all. Then one day Tia asked me if I wanted to join her and her young nephew Rhylee in the pool for a quick dip. Obviously, this was not going to be a 'proper' swim session, as the main purpose of this swim was to make sure Rhylee had a fun time. However, it did feel very strange to be gliding through the water again after such a long time away from it. It did make me wonder why I had not swum for almost a year!

The following month Cathy, Richard and I went for an anniversary swim at Milton Lake. The original plan was for the whole of 'Team West Suffolk' to get together for this, but it just proved too difficult to arrange with all our varied work patterns. So, in the end only half of the team met up. We had a pleasant swim followed by a BBQ, with Cathy's partner April and their boisterous dog Harry also joining us for that part.

Then I stopped swimming again! I don't know why but I just never had any motivation to get my arse back in the pool/lake/sea and swim. Reflecting on these periods of non-swimming, it makes me wonder just how much I actually enjoy doing it. The thing is, while I'm actually swimming, especially in the sea, I really do feel great. It makes me feel alive and exhilarated. I prefer the sea to be a bit choppy as it adds to the fun. I love the feeling of the cold salty water against my skin and the slight unease of what may be lurking beneath me or what I may encounter. And on the occasion that you get a kiss from a jellyfish, it makes the adrenaline pump a bit faster, as the stinging sensation reminds you that they are still out there and may decide to strike again at any moment. It's all great fun! However, for some reason it appears that I only feel the urge to swim when I have something specific to aim for, and the North Channel had still not been mentioned again since our journey back from France just over a year previously.

Another eight months passed, and it was now April 2019, when I received a call from Cathy asking if I fancied a swim at Felixstowe. Obviously, I said yes straight away and couldn't wait to get back in the sea. This did make me puzzle over the fact that in the twenty-one months since our relay swim I had only swum three times. I simply couldn't think why this was the case and actually felt ashamed that I had allowed this to happen.

I pulled up in the car park next to Cathy's car and we both got out and greeted each other. We chatted while we got changed into our swimwear, and as I stood there fiddling with my goggles, I noticed Cathy putting her wetsuit on.

"You got your wetsuit?" I exclaimed.

"Yeah, we said on the phone we would wear them as it's still only April," Cathy replied.

"Oh, I don't remember, and I didn't bring mine."

"Well, you'll just have to get cold," Cathy said with a smug kind of chuckle.

I just want to point out the reason we wear wetsuits when the water is colder is not because we are wimps, it's because we live some distance from the sea and without wetsuits, we would have a very limited time in the water. A wetsuit simply means we can spend longer swimming in the sea and therefore make our long journey worthwhile.

I was beginning to feel I was at a distinct disadvantage for not having my wetsuit with me but at the same time I knew I just needed to throw myself back into this sea swimming lark and get on with it. The water was only 10°C but we managed thirty minutes in there. Obviously for me, the obligatory shakes started soon after exiting the water and they lasted for some time. I am well known for being a 'great shaker' after cold-water swims. People often ask me why I shake so much after my swims; after all I'm a solo English Channel swimmer so surely I must be used to the cold? Yes, I am used to the cold and I embrace it and even enjoy it, but my body reacts the way it does, and I have no control over that.

Once back at the car and getting dry, Cathy said something to me which stopped me dead in my tracks. "So, was that our first training swim for the North Channel?"

Deep down I knew this moment was going to come but I was just never quite sure when it would happen. I cannot remember the reply I gave, maybe because I was too focused on what Cathy had just said to me. But I knew this was the start point of another crazy journey for the pair of us. A journey that would be tough, challenging and hopefully fun at times, but most importantly successful. Obviously, I knew it would also involve others and hoped it would be the rest of our channel relay team that would join us on this adventure, but at the same time, I accepted the fact that this may not be the case. I arrived home that evening feeling somewhat excited but also a little unsettled at the thought of what I may have to go through over the next couple of years or so.

About seven weeks later I had a missed call from Cathy while I was at work. It was the call I had been expecting and, in my own little warped kind of way, looking forward to. The following day we managed to both be available at the same time to speak. I knew after the small talk it would be a discussion about a North Channel relay swim and I was happy about that. After all, I had had enough time to get used to the idea. I didn't hesitate to agree that I was up for it. However, I got the feeling that Cathy was simply prompting me to take control and organize it. I suppose having been the team captain for our English Channel relay, this was a natural assumption that Cathy would make. It had been particularly stressful for me organizing our channel relay race with two teams, even though I had a lot of help, and I simply wanted to take a bit of a step back on this one. I explained this to Cathy and asked if she was willing to take over as team captain. There was only a slight hesitation, maybe because she wasn't expecting me to suggest it, but to my delight she agreed to be our next captain. I was so happy about this as I knew she would make an excellent captain and she was certainly a very worthy one. Once again it was just Cathy and I that had started to form a swim team and it was now time to begin recruiting the other members of our channel relay team and hope that they would join us for this next big challenge.

I was straight on the internet and was soon looking at the 'North Channel Swimming Association' website. My good friend Maggie Kidd was the secretary and so I messaged her to discuss it. Maggie was thrilled that we may be taking on this swim and offered her full support. Maggie was the second woman to ever swim the North Channel solo back in 1988. She had swum it the day after Alison Streeter who also held the world record for the most English Channel swims until 2021, when Chloë McCardel took the title by completing forty-four crossings.

The next thing we needed to do was convince the others that this was a great swim for us to attempt together. So, I messaged

Tia, Ria, Richard and George to see what they thought about the plan. George replied and agreed straight away to join us, whereas Richard wanted more information before making a decision. Tia unfortunately declined as she said she was thinking about starting a family and so obviously wouldn't be able to commit. If I'm honest, I was half expecting this reply from Tia, and although we were very disappointed that she wouldn't be a part of the team, we were also thrilled for her and her partner Joel that they had their own exciting adventure ahead of them. Ria was away on holiday at the time I messaged her and so it was a while before I received her reply. When she did reply she said she wasn't sure if she could commit and needed a little bit more time to think about it, which was fair enough.

An ex-colleague of mine called Kerrie was a keen swimmer and was also a lifeguard prior to joining the ambulance service. I first met Kerrie after we had already organized both teams for our channel relay race and at the time, she told me she would have loved to have been a part of our team. She had asked me to please consider her for any future challenges. Naturally I contacted Kerrie to see if she was interested in joining us and she agreed.

Around the same time, Cathy told me about one of her best friends from school called Megan and how she thought she would make a great member of the team. After some discussion I agreed that Megan should join us if Ria was not able to. Obviously, I didn't know Megan at all and so I had to trust in Cathy's judgement as to whether she was suitable. Luckily, I did know Cathy well enough to have this amount of trust in her. Oh, and just to add a bit more to the mix – Megan was pregnant. Yes, this potential new member of the team was not only a complete unknown to me, but she had yet to give birth before this swim as well as everything else becoming a new parent entails. But still I had no doubt in Cathy's decision to have Megan on the team, and although having never met Megan, for some reason I totally believed in her, and had no doubt she could deliver the goods, and I don't just mean a baby. At this point we were still awaiting a definite decision from Ria and so Megan's possible place on the team relied on this.

Ria didn't keep us dangling for too long and, unfortunately, she also told me she was unable to commit and therefore would not be joining the team. I was very sad that both Tia and Ria would not be a part of our new swimming challenge but totally understood their reasons. In the meantime, Cathy had discussed the proposal with Megan, who was up for joining us, and so with Ria pulling out and Megan joining us as a certain, we now had a full team of six swimmers.

However, only a few days later, Kerrie messaged me to say she had given the idea a lot more thought and didn't think she would have the time to train for such a challenge. After a long discussion, I soon realized her mind was made up and she would not be a part of our team. So now we were back down to five members.

Then I thought of another swimmer who may well be up for it. A good friend of mine who had also done a solo English Channel swim the same year I did mine. In fact, she had now completed two solo English Channel swims plus a couple of channel relays. I also remembered a conversation we once had where we agreed it would be great to do a relay together sometime in the future. It was time to contact Sam Jones to see if she was willing to join us. I obviously spoke to Cathy first and also asked for the approval of George and Richard as they all knew Sam from when she was part of the boat crew on *Suva* during our channel relay. They all agreed that with her experience she would make an excellent member of the team.

I contacted Sam and put the idea to her. She loved the idea of doing a relay swim with us all but straight away said she did not want to do the North Channel. This did come as a bit of a surprise to me to be honest, but then when she explained her reasons, I did understand where she was coming from. Sam laughed and said maybe if we were swimming to the Scilly Isles or something then she may join us. I explained Sam's thoughts about why she did not want to swim the North Channel to the rest of the team. It was now a choice of continuing to look for another team member, go with a team of five, or come up with another swim challenge.

This unexpected turbulence within plans had made me ponder over what our next challenge should be and I couldn't help thinking about Sam's flippant remark about swimming to the Scilly Isles. It was strange that Sam had mentioned this because I had actually looked into this swim several years previously. Back then I had researched swims from mainland Britain to the Isles of Scilly. I already knew that it had been accomplished as a solo swim by Alison Streeter and Beth French but I was looking to see if a relay team had ever achieved it. Despite a thorough search, I found no mention of any relay completing this swim.

I decided to research this swim further. The next thing I did was message Vicky Middlemast (Miller). Vicky was a fellow solo English Channel swimmer and we were friends on Facebook; I also knew she had recently made an attempt at a swim from the Scilly Isles to Cornwall. Unfortunately, Vicky managed twenty-six of the twenty-eight miles before the swim was aborted, but it was an awesome attempt. Vicky gave me the contact details of the escort boat she used, *Celtic Fox*. I then messaged the pilot, Mark Johns, of *Celtic Fox* to make some enquiries. Mark told me that as far as he knew, no relay team had ever completed the swim.

I called Cathy and suggested the idea of this alternative swim and it didn't take me very long at all to sell it to her. The general feeling between the two of us was that the North Channel had already been achieved by a relay, whereas a relay swim to the Isles of Scilly was yet to be conquered. We both decided the North Channel will always be there for a future swim, so maybe we should put that on the back burner and go for a world first relay swim to the Isles of Scilly.

We discussed this idea with the rest of the team and they all appeared to be really up for this new challenge. All we needed to do was convince Sam to join us to complete our team.

A few days later, on a lovely Sunday afternoon, I was out walking in the warm sun when I decided it was time to call Sam for a chat. We spoke for a while, well Sam more than me, and then I dropped the bombshell. I asked if she would join our relay team if we were going to be attempting a swim to the Isles of Scilly. There was only a small amount of persuasion involved I seem to remember. Sam agreed and I could not wait to tell the rest of the team that she was going to join us for this new epic challenge. We now had a team of six and an exciting possible world first swim to achieve. I simply could not wait to get stuck into this one!

THREE

THE JOURNEY BEGINS

Although I was extremely disappointed that the whole of my original team were not joining us on this next adventure, at the same time I was excited to see how our two new members would fit in and how we would all perform together. Megan had now given birth to a gorgeous little boy called Owen and she had such a tough journey ahead of her. How she managed to juggle the difficulty of being a new mother with training for our relay is totally beyond my comprehension. What this did show, however, was that Megan was as hardcore as Cathy had said she was.

So, let me introduce the team. Sam is a mother to two grown-up sons. She works as a boat skipper and has also accomplished two solo English Channel swims so has a huge amount of experience both on and in the sea. Sam has also run a couple of marathons with me.

Richard works in the car sales industry and also has a lot of experience both in and on the water. He has been sailing since he was very young and we were also both members of the Bury St Edmunds swimming club as kids, so I have known Richard the longest out of all the members of the team. He is married with two grown-up daughters.

George is also married with two grown-up daughters, but what he actually does for a living is still a bit of a mystery. I first met George (or Darren as I knew him then as that is his real name) back in 1999 when I had just started out as a student ambulance technician. It was my third shift on an ambulance that I was crewed to work with George in Ipswich. He was already a paramedic and we seemed to get on well. A year or so later, George became a team leader and was my line manager. After leaving the ambulance service, George went to work for the local Care Commissioning Group (CCG). It has become a bit of a running joke between Cathy and I that we are determined to find out what he now actually does for a living. But after several years of questioning him and even after spending a whole week with him in Cornwall for this swim, we are still none the wiser! We joke with him that he does meetings for a living but I'm sure there must be more to it than that. George is also a very strong and consistent open-water swimmer and obviously was a part of our English Channel relay swim.

Megan now has her young son Owen with her partner Mark and she has quite a rare job as a cardiac perfusionist. She was the least experienced member of the team when it comes to open-water swimming but we never doubted her for a second.

Cathy is married to April and we first met when she started work as a student paramedic. I remember very clearly the first time I was ever crewed with Cathy and that conversation we had about swimming across the English Channel. She was immediately so keen on the idea of this massive challenge and this made a huge impact on me. I instantly knew that Cathy should be the first member of my English Channel relay team and again it was Cathy and I who were the organizers of this latest challenge. Cathy now works as a winch paramedic for the coastguard down in Kent. I feel so proud of where that young student has directed her career.

So that just leaves me. I'm married to Cherie and we have two sons and a daughter. They are now grown-up and have all done us proud. I have previously completed a solo English Channel swim, as well as organizing two teams to race across the English Channel.

While communicating with Mark Johns, the skipper of *Celtic Fox*, he told me that another relay team had been booked with him that year for a relay attempt to the Isles of Scilly but were forced to pull out. He also said he only had one more slot available for 2020 which was at the end of September. While I was still trying to get my head around the idea of our team possibly attempting this challenge the following year, Mark messaged me to say the other team that had cancelled the previous year had now booked that last slot for 2020. I was gutted that they had beaten us to booking this swim, but at the same time slightly relieved, because it took the pressure off us all making that decision to go for the swim the following year, with minimal preparation. This meant it would give us more time to train and organize everything, but it also meant we may not be the first relay team to complete this swim. I messaged the team with the news and there were mixed emotions all round.

In the meantime, I happened to be chatting online to a fellow English Channel swimmer friend of mine. During our conversation, she asked me if I had any future swims planned. Although still very early days, I told her about our possible plans to do a relay from mainland England to the Isles of Scilly. Her reply shocked me! Apparently, this friend was a member of the team that had cancelled the previous year and had now rebooked for 2020. This was an all-female, four-person relay team, but their swim had to be abandoned in 2019 due to her contracting glandular fever and another team member having problems with her back.

I informed the others of the situation regarding the other relay team that had taken the last slot for 2020. Sam was also friends with this swimmer. We had discussions about what this may mean for us hoping to achieve a world-first swim. Firstly, the other team had to go ahead with the swim that they had already cancelled once. Secondly, and most importantly, they had to be successful. Obviously, we were supportive of their attempt and hoped they would succeed, as this is simply the nature of the open-water swimming community; we support and encourage each other. However, this also meant that if they succeeded, we would no longer be the first relay to achieve this swim. If we did manage to complete it, we would still be the first six-person relay team and the first mixed sex team to accomplish this challenge. We even spoke about swimming it in the other direction – from the Isles of Scilly to mainland England. There were other options open to us. However, being the very first relay team was still our ultimate goal and what we had set our hearts on, but we had to accept that this may no longer be achievable.

Now that Cathy was the team captain, I passed on to her the contact details for Mark Johns so that she could liaise with him directly to organize a date for our swim and conduct all the other arrangements that would be required. Possible dates were put forward to the rest of the team for 2021 for us to consider and plan alongside our busy work schedules. We knew the other team were booked for their attempt the previous year and we did wonder if they may pull out again and book for the same year as us, but earlier in the season. Despite this possibility, the only date we could all agree on was in mid-September. Obviously, this would give the other team a chance to postpone from 2020 and still get a slot before us in 2021, but we had no control over that and we had to do what was right for us. We agreed that we should book our swim window from 14th to 18th September.

Around this time, I remember putting a message on our group chat suggesting that it was time to think of a name for our team. I was already thinking it should be short and to the point. Our previous team was called 'Team West Suffolk'. I believe I chose this name because, on that occasion, we had two teams competing and we had to have names to distinguish between the two teams – the other team being 'Team East Suffolk'. I liked the idea of a three-word team name. I believed it should contain the word 'Scilly' as that was our destination. Obviously, there were six of us and we were going to be swimming. As I was in the process of mulling this all over in my head, Richard replied to my message with his idea for a name – 'Scilly Six Swimmers'. Straight away I knew Richard and I were thinking along the same lines, but it just didn't feel quite right to me. Before I even had a chance to reply to Richard's idea, Sam put another suggestion on the chat, and I assume it was prompted by Richard's idea – 'Six Scilly Swimmers'. That was it! Instantly I knew that this had to be our team name. Nobody even attempted to come up with anything better because I don't think they could. It was time for 'Six Scilly Swimmers' to get out there and do some serious training for this monumental swim.

Just as we were about to start training for this huge challenge, something very strange happened. We were all suddenly put into 'lockdown' by the government due to a virus that was doing its rounds. We were told that we were only allowed to go out of the house for essentials. Swimming pools were closed and people were not even allowed to swim in the open sea. This was such a bizarre situation and nothing like I had ever experienced before. This 'lockdown' meant that I, as well as the rest of the team, were simply not allowed to train for our relay swim. We had to stay at home and make the best of what we had. What we had was not the sea or any open water or even a pool. We had pretty much nothing on offer that would help us achieve our goal. It did cross my mind if I should suggest to the team whether we should consider putting the swim off for another year due to our lack of training opportunities but then I thought about each individual member of the team and what their possible reply would be. I just knew this hardcore team would all say 'NO'! Lockdown would never stop us; in fact, nothing would stop this team.

During this first lockdown, my friend on the other team messaged me to say they would obviously have to cancel their Scilly swim attempt for 2020 due to not being able to train for it. This was totally understandable and I did feel really bad for them as this was so out of their control. However, there was still opportunity for them to rebook their slot before us in 2021 if they wished to.

Eventually, we were allowed back into open water again but then Sam messaged me with some bad news. She told me how she had tripped on a rope at work and managed to sustain a spiral fracture of her left tibia. Spiral fractures are messy at the best of times and this unexpected injury would obviously put Sam's training on hold for the foreseeable future and all we could do was hope that she mended quickly. However, this was not to be the case at all, and Sam would face surgery and several complications on her very long road to recovery.

In July I met up with Cathy and her friend Rebecca for a swim at Felixstowe, which was my first swim that year. This was a relatively short swim and I knew it was now time to start cracking on with some serious training now that we were allowed back into the water.

Around this time, Richard took a break down in Cornwall with his family and met up with Sam for a swim. Sam's leg was still not great and was causing her pain while swimming. This was a huge concern for the team and we all hoped that Sam's leg would repair so she could get back to some proper training.

August arrived and then something terrible and very unexpected happened. I was having a nice peaceful evening with Cherie and Phoebe while Sean was upstairs playing online games with his friends. Cherie was reading an old diary out to Phoebe and I, and I found one particular bit really funny. So funny that I just could not stop laughing! Cherie and Phoebe were laughing too and Cherie did her usual thing of turning away so she couldn't see me, as this made her laugh even more. Apparently, she laughs more when she sees me laughing. I remember laughing so much I had trouble catching my breath, and that was the last thing I remember before coming round with Cherie resuscitating me and shaking me in desperation. What the hell was going on? I was confused. I didn't know what was happening. I looked over to see Phoebe in tears and on her phone. She was talking to the emergency services and asking for help.

Cherie told me I had stopped breathing and had gone from a red/purple colour, to a clammy grey/yellow colour and then to a distinct shade of blue. Apparently, they thought it was 'all over' for me when I wasn't responding to her initial attempt to get me back. I simply couldn't fathom what was happening. The whole scene seemed very chaotic and emotionally charged. It was a far cry from the happy and jovial moment we had been sharing, what seemed to me like just a couple of seconds earlier. I found it really difficult to accept what I was being told and insisted I was fine and there was nothing wrong with me. I told Phoebe to tell them on the phone that I was alright and that I no longer needed an ambulance. The last thing I wanted was some old colleagues of mine to turn up and start fussing over me.

In hindsight I was a fool! Of course, I should have been checked out medically at the time but, being a paramedic, I was obviously very persuasive and convinced Cherie and Phoebe that I didn't need any help. The rest of the evening was a very sober affair as I ruminated over the whole situation, and I guess Cherie and Phoebe were also doing the same. I played it over and over in my head and tried to make some kind of sense of it, but I simply couldn't process it properly. I was hoping it had been a simple faint, but hearing the in-depth descriptions of what had happened from Cherie and Phoebe, this was clearly not the case. It was a definite respiratory arrest that lasted over a minute. I wasn't breathing and was starting to turn blue. I can't imagine how scary this must have been for the both of them. Even though it concerned me greatly, it was still some time before I eventually sought medical assistance and had tests done. The tests showed nothing, but then I was expecting that to be the case considering I had left it so long. Having been a paramedic for two decades, I knew all too well that incidents like these needed to be investigated immediately to give the best chance of finding a cause. Maybe I was just too scared to face the truth at the time.

Following this incident, I was obviously very concerned that I did not know the reason for my sudden respiratory arrest, but I also knew that I could not let this define me or constrain me in any way, and I would have to just get back out there and start training again. A week later I met up with Richard and George for a swim in Cambridge at the Jesus Green Lido. I was really looking forward to finally getting to swim in this outdoor pool as I had originally intended to do some of my training there back in 2008 in preparation for my solo English Channel swim. For various reasons I never got to do this at the time but now I finally had the chance to swim in this iconic pool.

Before getting in the water, we had to take our obligatory selfie shot to send to our WhatsApp group to prove to the others that we were training. This had become quite a thing between us and it had led to much banter. A few weeks earlier, Cathy and I had posted a picture of us at Felixstowe following our swim. It was a simple photo of the two of us standing in the sea in our swimwear. However, Sam brought up the fact that we were not wearing swim hats or had goggles. In her words, "No swim hat, no goggles, didn't happen!"

We were now fully aware that any swim photos we took would have to include our full swim attire, otherwise it was seen as suspicious and wouldn't count. So, we all posed in our swim hats and holding our goggles. George held his phone up to take the shot and then he commented that he may need a wide-angle lens to fit me in! We laughed at his comment but it resonated with me because I knew that my respiratory arrest the previous week had been a huge wake-up call for me. It was the wake-up call that I needed and welcomed with open arms. It was following this respiratory arrest that I had weighed myself and found that I was the heaviest I had ever been in my life. Looking at the photo of Phoebe and I, taken on her 21st birthday during our trip to Overstrand just a few weeks previously, I knew I had put far too much weight on and seriously needed to lose a good stone or more.

I was obviously very apprehensive about getting back in the water following my incident and I couldn't help thinking that if it happened again while I was swimming, it could be a lot more serious. The three of us chatted about my experience and I explained that I was going to take it very easy as I was still testing the water, so to speak. Then George told us that he too would have to take it easy as he had been suffering from a shoulder cuff injury for some time and was having physio for it. I knew how painful this type of injury could be as I had the same problem in the lead-up to my solo English Channel swim and had extensive physio on it to help me achieve the swim.

Then I suddenly saw the funny side of it all. Here we had a team of six swimmers who were hoping to achieve a very difficult world-first swim in just twelve months' time. Lockdown had prevented us from training as much as we needed to. Sam was still suffering and not yet recovered from her fractured tibia; George had a shoulder cuff injury that he was receiving treatment for; and I recently had a respiratory arrest with an unknown cause. I couldn't help thinking that we weren't the healthiest team out there and wondered just how on Earth we were going to pull this one off!

I jumped into the pool and it was bloody cold. After all these years, why did the water still feel so cold? Then I looked to the far end of the pool and it seemed like such a long distance away. When I was pool training, I was used to the usual 25m length; however, this lido was a staggering 91m. It was the longest pool I had ever swum in. I cautiously began swimming my first length and, apart from feeling very unfit, I was fine. After a couple of lengths, I felt my confidence growing again and so I upped the pace slightly. I felt like I had overcome a milestone. It would have been all too easy for me to have pulled out of this relay following my respiratory arrest, claiming that I simply wasn't medically fit to take on such a challenge. But that's certainly not what I wanted to do, and although I'm sure the rest of the team would have totally understood my reasons for pulling out, I knew they wouldn't want me to either. I couldn't live the rest of my life ruled by the fear of 'what if it happens again'? I just had to crack on with it and stay positive.

I didn't cover a huge distance that evening, but I did feel like I had turned a corner and I saw it as my first proper training session for our relay. Now it seemed to me that the journey had properly begun and it filled me with excitement.

However, it wasn't just the swimming I had to train for but also running. My mum had paid for me to run the Brighton Marathon in April 2020 as it happened to fall on my 50th birthday and I was keen to celebrate my milestone birthday by running this iconic marathon. Then Covid came along and the Brighton Marathon was postponed until April 2021. Following further restrictions and guidelines it was postponed again until the 12th of September 2021. This was just three days before our swim window started for our relay swim. I did give this whole situation a lot of thought, as the last thing I would want to do was put our relay swim at risk in any way. I figured that the worst-case scenario was that I would have buggered my legs up following my marathon, but my main driving force while swimming came from my arms and upper body and they should not be affected by a long run. So, I decided I should go ahead with Brighton. It was beginning to look like I would be having a very busy week in September 2021.

FOUR

WALLY

It was just over a month following my respiratory arrest when I decided I should attempt some kind of running. Obviously, a short run would be the safest way to begin, and Cherie insisted that I should not run alone, just in case something happened, so we both got up very early one morning and headed out onto the street for a very slow 1.3-mile jog around the estate. I felt very unfit and was struggling from the start. Cherie ran beside me and I felt bad that I was holding her back on what could be a proper training run for her. As I plodded my way around the pavement I had to question if I should be running at all, and I also had that conversation in my mind about whether I should continue with my training to run the Brighton Marathon.

The last time I had such negative thoughts about my running was following my first half-marathon when I had completely messed my knee up. It was only due to the positivity and amazing work that my physiotherapist Jo had done with me that I was not only able to continue running but was also able to complete several marathons and a hundred-mile ultra-run. Deep down there somewhere in my head, there is someone or something that keeps shouting at me to just carry on no matter what!

Cherie and I finished our short run without any dramas and that was the best I was hoping for. All I had to do now was to gradually build up to a level where I could complete a marathon again. This seemed to be such a huge mountain to climb but, as always, I would break it down into manageable chunks so that it would not feel like an overwhelming and impossible task.

Richard, George and I only managed two swims at the Jesus Green Lido before it closed for the winter and Richard and I also sneaked in a swim at Milton Lake before they too closed. Felixstowe was our nearest point for sea swimming, but because of the distance and the relatively short time we could spend in the water at that time of the year, it simply wasn't worth the journey. So, we would be forced to continue our training in an indoor pool until such time that we could get back out into the open water again. Sam was the lucky one as she lived close to the sea and so was able to maintain her open-water exposure throughout the winter months. The rest of us returned to open-water swimming as soon as we could the following year.

The team had some discussions about using our swim as a platform to raise money for a good cause. It didn't take very long at all to agree on a charity, and that was the Royal National Lifeboat Institution (RNLI). There were obvious reasons why this would be an ideal charity to raise money for, but it was also very close to Sam's heart as she used to be a lifeboat volunteer in Dover.

In January 2021, I set up a JustGiving page and almost immediately people started to donate money. I always find that once you commit to raising money for a charity, then it makes everything more real and suddenly the pressure is on. It is no longer some whimsical idea or fantasy about achieving something huge but something that you are telling the world about and asking people to hand over money for in support of your crazy pursuit. Now we would simply have to achieve our goal, or else we would be not only letting ourselves down but others too, and that was something none of us were prepared to do.

The time had also come for us to think about some kind of team clothing and a team logo. Richard had a business contact, Oliver Hilton, at a company called Precision. He told Oliver about our upcoming relay swim and he very kindly offered a donation to provide us with hoodies and T-shirts. He also offered to design our team logo for us. Any money that was left over would go straight to our charity. Oliver provided us with six different designs for hoodies and T-shirts, which were all great, but between us we chose the one we liked the best.

This was a lovely gesture of goodwill, and having these tops would help us to feel like we were more connected and part of a team. We all knew that in reality it was very unlikely that the whole team would all get together before the big day. It was easy for Richard, George and I to meet up to swim as we all lived in Bury St Edmunds and within a five-minute drive from each other. Cathy lived a short drive away just over the border in Essex. However, Megan lived way up north and Sam lived down on the south coast. We all had very busy jobs and most of us did shift work. Due to the sheer distance and availability of all the team members, we had to accept that team building would have to be done at a distance. I knew this was more than possible as it was a similar situation during the preparation for our English Channel relay swim in 2017. Back then we didn't even have distance as a factor because we all lived within a half hour drive from each other. It was simply a matter of not all being available at the same time to meet up. The first time the whole team got together on that occasion was the night before the swim itself.

The other thing we needed to think about was making the swim official. This was very important to us because it was such a huge challenge and we obviously wanted it to count and be taken seriously. With English Channel swims there were two well-established organizations to observe and ratify swims. These were the Channel Swimming Association (CSA) and the Channel

Swimming and Piloting Federation (CS&PF). We wanted to do our swim using English Channel swimming rules, but obviously neither of these organizations would be able to provide pilots and observers, so we would have to look elsewhere. As mentioned earlier, this swim had already been done twice by solo swimmers using English Channel swimming rules (and a third using a wetsuit). From what I understand, none of these swims had official observers during the swim itself. There was clearly no organization that dealt specifically with swims between Cornwall and the Isles of Scilly, so naturally, I contacted the British Long Distance Swimming Association (BLDSA) and explained what our intention was. They replied saying they were happy to provide observers for our swim and, if successful, they would officially ratify it. As this was an inaugural swim, we would require two observers.

My Brighton Marathon training was not going as well as I hoped it would. Firstly, I was having my usual intermittent issues with my knees. I could never predict which knee would decide to give me problems but every so often one of them would cause me some pain while running, often making me limp-run back home. Sometimes this pain could last a few days or so. It was very unsettling and I longed to be able to just enjoy running without this constant threat at the back of my mind.

On top of this I finally got my appointment through for the first of my two planned varicose vein operations. The first surgery was to be on my right leg. I was having ablation on a large vein. This basically meant having an incision made just below my knee and a metal wire pushed up into the vein all the way to my groin. After a series of local anaesthetic injections all along the route, sections of the wire a few centimeters at a time would be heated to 120°C to burn that part of the vein. I didn't anticipate this to be a pleasant procedure, but my biggest concern was how this would affect my training for my marathon and maybe the relay swim also.

The operation was due to take place on June 1st, and because of all the Covid protocols, this meant I had to have a Covid test three days before and then self-isolate until the procedure. This just happened to fall on a lovely sunny bank holiday weekend, and I absolutely hated having to be confined to my home while everyone else was enjoying the hot weather with friends and family at the beach or having a BBQ.

It had been nearly twenty years since I first spoke to my GP with concerns about my varicose veins. He had dismissed it at the time and went on about how the NHS has more important things to spend its money on. So I pretty much gave up on the idea of having them treated. Then one day I had to make an appointment to see a GP as my depression had once again spiraled out of control. I saw a new doctor whom I had never met before. She was amazing. She actually took the time to sit there and look me in the eye and properly listen to me and understand my situation. I knew medication once again was inevitable, but as she typed out my prescription, she said something I've never heard a GP say before. She told me the meds were only a short-term fix and she wanted to help me come off them as soon as possible. She asked that I see her every month to review my mood with a view to easing me back off the medication. Usually, people are put on antidepressants indefinitely, but this doctor clearly knew that this was not best practice and wanted me off them again as soon as I was able to.

A couple of months later at the end of one of these reviews, I was just about to leave when she again said something I've never heard a GP say before. "While you're here, is there anything else I can help you with?"

I was shocked that she said this, as GPs usually only deal with one problem per visit and can't wait to get you out of the door. I hesitated for a moment and then told her I had been having issues with varicose veins for many years but, apparently, I was low priority. Straight away she asked to have a look and she couldn't believe I had not been treated. As she explained, if it's NHS money they were worried about then it's very short-sighted because the complications from untreated varicose veins would ultimately cost the NHS far more than early prevention. She prescribed some cream for me which she said would not work but they'd be unable to accept a referral unless an alternative had already been tried.

I returned the following month to confirm the cream had made no difference and so she made a referral then and there. If it wasn't for Dr Unsworth, I would definitely still be waiting for my veins to be treated. Sadly, for me and many other patients, this fabulous GP left my surgery to work at Addenbrookes hospital. It was our loss, but they gained a great doctor. If only all GPs could be like her.

June 1st arrived and I was feeling quite anxious about the procedure. I had to be at the day surgery unit quite early, so I left in good time for the two-mile walk to the hospital. Obviously, I would not be able to drive afterwards, so the plan was that Cherie would come to the hospital and, if I was able to, we would get the bus home. If not, we would simply order a taxi.

I had a quick assessment by a nurse and was then led to a cubicle where I was given a gown to put on. I then sat there and waited. There were five other men in my bay waiting for some kind of surgical procedure. Surgeons started coming in to talk to them and get consent forms signed. Before long I was the only one who had not been spoken to. I was beginning to think they had forgotten about me. Then the ward Sister came over to me and explained that my surgery had been postponed as my surgeon had just found out a family member had Covid and so was self-isolating. I was gutted as I had not only psyched myself up for my operation but had also spent the entire bank holiday weekend isolating for nothing! I got myself dressed and called Cherie to tell her the news and then took a slow walk home.

I was very quickly sent a new appointment for my operation, and it was June 28th, so I didn't have too long to wait. Again, I had to have a Covid swab taken and then self-isolate for the three days prior to the procedure. This time my surgery was an afternoon slot, so I had plenty of time to prepare myself; however, during the morning, I had a call from the day surgery unit explaining that my operation had to be cancelled as my surgeon had just had a death in the family. I couldn't help thinking my surgeon was a very unlucky man and hoped that when he did finally get to work on me, his luck would change. I also couldn't help wondering if the reasons they were giving for my cancelled procedures were just taken from a 'list of excuses' that they had. Obviously, these would be excuses that nobody could really argue with or complain about.

A while later I had yet another appointment sent through for July 27th. Third time lucky I hoped. Following yet another three days of self-isolation, the day finally arrived, and I half expected that phone call to say it was cancelled because my surgeon had been eaten by an alligator or abducted by aliens, but thankfully it never came.

My surgery wasn't the most pleasant experience to go through, but I was just glad that I was finally getting the problem sorted. There was only one little glitch, where all of a sudden, I felt intense burning inside my leg, like it was on fire. I had been warned this was a possibility and to tell them immediately if it happened. The surgeon quickly turned the heat off and I was given another injection of anaesthetic before they continued.

We all chatted while the procedure was under way and at one point I happened to mention that I was running the Brighton Marathon in less than seven weeks. This comment caused a certain amount of laughter among them and, clearly, they didn't think this would be a possibility. I wasn't phased by this as they obviously didn't know me.

Following the procedure, I was not allowed to run or swim for two weeks, which I obviously found very frustrating as there really wasn't much time to prepare for Brighton and then possibly three days later having to take part in our Scilly swim relay. I wanted to be doing some serious training but instead I had to make do with daily walks. Even when I was allowed to start running again, I was told to be cautious as I had to give my veins time to reroute themselves to get my blood flowing more efficiently up my legs and back to my heart.

I really could have done without this surgery being done so close to our big swim and my marathon, but I had to treat it as just another obstacle to overcome. If it prevented me from running the Brighton Marathon, I would be gutted but these things happen sometimes. The one thing it would not prevent me from doing was our Scilly relay swim. That was always a dead certainty for me. Even if I couldn't walk, I would still be getting in the sea and doing my part for the team.

The time had also come for us to have a group chat about the finances of the swim. Richard agreed to be in charge of the bank account to pay for the boat while Megan had taken on the task of arranging our accommodation. She had chosen a lovely town house in the heart of Penzance that would easily accommodate those travelling down with a spare room for Sam if she wished to stay over.

We were also trying to arrange a team meet-up in Clacton for a swim. It would have been amazing to get the whole team together for this, but we all knew it would be unlikely. We finally came up with June 18th as the date to meet up in Clacton. Sam would not be able to make it as it was simply too far for her, and she had far too much going on anyway. As it got closer to the day, Richard informed us that he too would be unable to come along due to work commitments. So that left four of us and we were looking forward to spending the day together and having a swim or two. However, the weather had other plans for us, and the forecast given the day before was not looking very favourable. We still held out hope, but then on the day itself, the forecast had got worse and then lightning was predicted. Swimming was now out of the question, so it was agreed we should call it off and hope to arrange it for another day.

Around this time the national news shared a story that interested us all. Well, when I say 'interested' it was probably more concern than anything. The report told us about a walrus, nicknamed Wally, that had strayed from its native Arctic and traveled about 2500 miles along the west coast of Europe, taking in Spain, Wales and Cornwall. However, Wally had now taken up residence around St Mary's in the Isles of Scilly. This was the very place we were planning to finish our swim.

Wally was said to be around four years old and so still quite young. He also liked to play and had already destroyed several boats in the area. Although they said they didn't think he was a danger to humans, I'm not quite sure how much data they had to make such a bold claim, because I'm pretty certain they don't encounter humans very often in the Arctic. So obviously our main concern was bumping into Wally during our swim and him wanting to play with us. How does a 1000kg young walrus with massive tusks play with a human in the sea? It really wasn't something I wanted to contemplate too much and I tried to hide those thoughts in that safe place in my mind where I also keep sharks. And of course, there was also the risk of him deciding to climb on board the support boat and sinking it!

A month later Wally was still causing havoc, so they built a makeshift pontoon in St Mary's for him to climb on. There were two purposes for this pontoon. Firstly, to discourage Wally from climbing on boats and sinking them and secondly to help him rest and regain enough energy to return back home.

Wally seemed to capture the hearts of the nation and, despite the fact I didn't want to come face to face with him during my swim, I also fell in love with him. Nobody could blame him for destroying boats because the sea is his domain, and if us humans decide to venture into the sea where we don't naturally belong, then we can't complain when things don't go so well for us.

For me, Wally was an icon, and I made the suggestion to the rest of the team that we should 'adopt' him as our team mascot. Wally was all over the news and was currently residing in the very place we hoped to finish our relay. It all seemed so very logical and perfect to me. However, when I suggested it to the team, it went down like a lead balloon, and nobody supported this idea. I was actually quite shocked that none of my teammates could see the potential in this, but I had to respect their decision and so that idea was completely thrown out of the window, much to my disappointment.

June was a particularly difficult time for Sam as her father was very unwell and his condition had become terminal. Sam lived several hours away from where her father was in hospital and so she would have to stay away from home in order to be by his side. Sam spent as much time as she possibly could with her father and ensured that he was receiving the best possible care. We had been chatting a lot during this time and I could tell just how exhausted she had become, both physically and emotionally. Then one evening I was sitting at home watching television when I received a message from Sam which simply read "He's gone x".

I messaged Sam straight back with my condolences and also informed the rest of the team so that she didn't need to. The following day I had a long and emotional chat with Sam on the phone. Obviously, she was totally devastated but she was also having to remain strong as she had other family members to support and assist through this distressing time, especially her mother Sharon. Of course, there were also arrangements to be made.

All of the team would have completely understood if Sam had pulled out of the swim considering what she was going through and what she still had to go through. After all, training for our relay had obviously, and very understandably, fallen right to the bottom of her list of priorities. But Sam is no ordinary person. I knew she would pick herself up, deal with what she needed to and then just knuckle down and get on with it. And she would be doing it because that's exactly what her father would want her to do and expect of her.

FIVE

STEVE

In early July we became aware of another swim team that were attempting a relay swim from Cornwall to the Isles of Scilly. We did not know of such a team until they were already underway with their swim and posts were popping up on social media. This obviously came as a bit of a shock to us, even more so because they were using the same escort boat and pilot that we had booked for our swim. There had been no previous mention of this other team's attempt. As much as I wanted this team to succeed, I also remember feeling very deflated with the thought that if this team were successful then we would have missed out on the chance of becoming the first to complete this swim. However, as we began to observe photos and videos of their attempt in progress, it quickly became apparent that this was a very different type of swim altogether. For a start, this was clearly a wetsuit swim and we would obviously be following English Channel swimming rules and therefore strictly no wetsuits. It also later became apparent (having read a report on their swim) that fins were also used and the timings of each swimmer's turn in the water were very random. There was no official observer and they were clearly not following any kind of recognized rules. There was actually very little comparison between their swim and what we were aiming to achieve. Yes, they were a group of swimmers who successfully started a relay in Cornwall and finished in the Isles of Scilly, which was a wonderful achievement and they raised a lot of money for charity in the process, but we were doing something very different. We could now relax a bit, knowing that we had not been beaten to the post. We still strived to be the very first non-wetsuit relay to swim to the Isles of Scilly adhering to strict English Channel swimming rules and be under the watchful eye of two official observers.

During May and early June, Richard, George and I trained several times at Lynford Lake which was a lovely place to swim in the evenings. The deep red reflection of the sun on the surface of the water looked totally magnificent and could be quite a distraction. We were usually the only swimmers in the water and it was a very peaceful and serene experience. However, lake swimming is all well and good but ideally, we needed to be out there in the sea. We needed salt water and waves and all the other little hazards that we may encounter, such as jellyfish and seaweed. So, from June

Richard, George and I training at Lynford Lake.

onwards we mostly headed over to Felixstowe for our evening swims. Felixstowe has always been a very special place for me as it was not just where my mum would take our family out for the day when we were kids, but it was also where I did much of my solo and relay English Channel training. I knew Felixstowe well and I was very used to its strong currents.

Most of the time we would start our swim at the beach hut where the Felixstowe Swimscapes Open Water Swimming folks would regularly meet up to swim. These are people from all walks of life who share one thing in common – open-water swimming. Once you are stripped down to your swimming trunks or costume and enter that cold salty water, all boundaries that often exist in everyday life between individuals just dissolve away. It doesn't matter what you do for a living, or how much money you have or don't have, once you are immersed in that water you are all equal, even if you are wrongly perceived as not being equal when on dry land. Organized by our friend Seamus Bennett, this is an amazing group of swimmers who not only enjoy the benefits of open-water swimming, but many have achieved great personal goals. From Seamus's beach hut we would usually swim to the pier and back which would normally take us a little over an hour. Sometimes we would swim under the pier and a little further, and then on the way back we would navigate around the end of the pier. I loved swimming around the pier as we appeared so far out from the shore, and then from the end of the pier we would take a direct route back to our start point. It was a great feeling gradually getting closer to the beach, as though we were finishing some important swim.

We also had another starting point at a beach hut a bit further down the promenade that belonged to our friend and my fellow English Channel solo swimmer Louise Stratford. From here we would join Louise, Amanda Bowden, Gilly Hoy and Louise's sister Abigail Brockwell for a social swim followed by a chat about our swimming plans. Sometimes chatting about swimming to others is as good as any training swim when it comes to motivation.

We usually liked to swim against the tide on the way out and then have the tide on our side on the return. This also meant we could not always swim to the pier if the tide was flowing in the other direction. On these occasions we would swim towards and then around a small peninsular called Cobbolds Point. This was always an exciting swim as the current around the end of Cobbolds Point was extremely fierce and you would be forced to swim like crazy to make any headway at all. It was like swimming on a treadmill and if you dared to stop at this point, you would be swept backwards at an alarming rate. The trick was to swim your heart out until you were just past the end point and then head back in towards the shore as quickly as possible where the current was a lot calmer and you could relax the pace again. Of course, the most enjoyable part was the journey back. Swimming around Cobbolds Point with the tide on your side was totally exhilarating. You would move through the water at such a great speed that it made you feel like you had super powers. Swimming around Cobbolds Point also brought back to me fond memories of training here with Tia and Ria for our English Channel relay. They both loved that speedy return swim.

On the 4th of August Cathy joined Richard, George and I in Felixstowe for an evening swim. It had not only been the first time the four of us had swum together since our English Channel relay four years previously, but it was also the largest gathering that we had managed of our current team. Obviously, there was no chance that Sam and Megan could also join us due to the sheer distance away that they lived. It was the Cobbolds Point route that we swum that evening and we also went out to the Cobbolds buoy before heading back to the beach.

Back in May I had received a message from a swimmer called Steven Andrew. He told me that he had an English Channel solo swim booked for September and that he had just started reading my first book about swimming the Channel, which his wife had bought him for Christmas. He said he could not believe the parallels between our swimming journeys. I have always been surprised at the amount of people that have told me this. However, Steve also told me that he lived in a village just outside Bury St Edmunds and so only a few miles from where I lived. He had also been training in the same pool that I used so we may have unknowingly already met.

Steve and I eventually arranged to meet up for an evening swim at Felixstowe at the end of August. George could not make it on this occasion so it would just be Richard and I that would join Steve in the sea, and we were looking forward to swimming with him.

That afternoon I packed my swimming bag and then walked the mile or so to where Richard worked. This was our usual routine when we went for an evening swim. Richard came out to meet me looking very smart in his shirt and tie while I stood outside his workplace in my shorts, sandals and vest top. I often wondered what Richard's colleagues thought about this strange man lurking outside their place of work, waiting for him to finish and then getting into his car to head off to goodness knows where. I actually found it a little amusing. So once again I got into Richard's car and we began our journey to Felixstowe, which would normally take about fifty minutes.

We were not that far from Felixstowe when I looked at my phone and noticed I had a message from Steve saying he was at the beach huts where we had planned to meet. However, this message had been sent about half hour previously but my phone had been on silent. My initial thought was that Steve was rather keen and had got there in very good time. Then a horrible feeling came over me and I checked the previous messages we had exchanged to arrange this rendezvous. To my horror I realized I had accidentally told him the wrong time and we were not going to get there for at least an hour after the time I had told him. I confessed my faux pas to

Richard and felt like a complete fool. I replied to Steve with my apologies but guessed he had probably already started his swim without us.

Richard and I pulled up on the promenade and I got straight out of the car and began looking for Steve, just in case he was still hanging on for us. There was no sign of him so I assumed he was somewhere out there in the sea. I felt really bad that I had told him the wrong time. My next mission was to get out there in the sea and find Steve to apologize and explain how I had messed up.

There didn't appear to be that many swimmers in the sea that evening. We passed a few but I didn't think they were Steve. Richard and I stopped periodically to have a quick chat and shared the same view that if Steve was swimming the same route that we were, to the pier and back, then we had definitely not passed him by.

Eventually we were approaching the pier and I spotted another swimmer who was just returning from it. It had to be Steve, I thought, and so I started swimming towards him. As I got closer, I stopped and looked up and he did the same. All I could see through my slightly misted goggles was what appeared to be a male head bobbing about in the sea with a swim hat on. I shouted over to him, "Are you Steve?"

"No," he replied, "I'm Andy!"

"Oh!"

I told Andy that I was pleased to meet him but I was actually looking for someone called Steve. He wished me good luck on my quest and continued swimming. I also got my head back down and started to swim again. It was then that the ridiculousness of the whole situation finally struck me. There I was swimming about in the North Sea, randomly looking for a man called Steve and the best I could do was find an Andy! It made me laugh and the more I thought about it the more I laughed. I simply couldn't stop. This was the very moment when I truly appreciated that laughter and swimming are not compatible!

As we were now on our return journey, I knew that I was not going to intercept Steve in the sea unless he was a very slow swimmer, which I doubted. Richard and I just had to swim back to our start point and hope that he was still there. As much as I love swimming in the sea, whenever I see the finish in sight it never fails to fill me with joy. Maybe this is because it is reminiscent of finishing epic swims. On this occasion I was hoping to finally get to meet Steve, whom I had clearly let down and wanted to personally apologize to.

Richard and I emerged from the water and carefully made our way up the stony beach, which is always a painful affair in bare feet. As we reached the promenade, a tall, slim figure with dark hair stood there with a huge smile on his face. It was Steve, who was now already dressed following his swim to the pier and back. Steve was very understanding about my incompetence and found it quite amusing.

A week later, and having finally got my act together with the arrangements, I actually got to swim with Steve. In fact, both Richard and George also made it that evening and we all had a great swim to the pier and back together. I was impressed with Steve's speed in the sea and this filled me with hope that he would make it to France on his big day.

From left: Steve, me, George and Richard.

SIX

ALMOST TIME

Our Scilly relay attempt was now just a matter of days away and the excitement was building. All the preparations had been made and all the training was done. Maybe some of us felt we hadn't trained as much as we would have liked, but circumstances had sometimes prevented us from doing more. We knew we must not let any negative thoughts manifest and take a hold. Positivity was the only way forward and would give us the very best chance of success.

Our swim window started on Wednesday 15th September and lasted for three days. Megan had booked our house from Sunday 12th for a week. Sam was going to be staying at home as she didn't have too far to travel to Penzance. All the others except me were travelling down on the Sunday. I was heading down on the Monday as I would be rather busy on Sunday with the small matter of running the Brighton Marathon. If it wasn't for this, I could have shared a lift with Richard and George.

I did think about driving to Brighton for my marathon and then driving straight from there to Penzance. In many ways this appeared to be the most logical thing to do. However, this would mean that Cherie would not be able to join me, and I wasn't keen on spending the weekend alone whilst taking part in such a huge event. This would also be followed by a long drive down to Cornwall with aching legs. On top of this, it would mean finding parking for an extra car while down there and having two cars travelling back to Bury St Edmunds at the end of the week, which seemed rather wasteful. So, I decided I would drive home after the marathon and then get the train to Penzance on the Monday morning. Luckily, I booked the train some time in advance and managed to get an extremely good deal.

Penzance was also where our escort boat, *Celtic Fox*, was moored. When it was time for our swim, *Celtic Fox* would take us along the coastline to our starting point at Nanjizal beach, and from there we would begin our journey to the Isles of Scilly.

The swim would start at the edge of the English Channel but we would soon find ourselves battling across the Atlantic Ocean. This was unknown territory for all of us with regards to swimming, and I was quite excited at the prospect of taking it on. We knew it would be different from swimming in the English Channel but until we were actually doing the swim, we wouldn't really know how exactly it would be different.

I had obviously researched the route we were taking and spent a lot of time looking at it on Google Maps to try to get my head around it and familiarize myself with the whole area. This may sound rather strange because, while I'd actually be swimming, I would simply be in cold salty water like I had been for years. However, I think it is very important to get to know the stretch of water as best you can before taking on a major swim. Study the start point and the potential finishing places. What else is out there? Would there be any possible landmarks, or to use the proper term, 'seamarks', when out at sea? These can be used as a focal point or even a source of comfort while swimming in the open sea.

There were a couple of notable seamarks that we might possibly see during our swim. At sea level, while actually swimming, it was unlikely we'd spot many at all unless they were very close, but whilst on the boat between swims, we would have a much better vantage point.

Wolf Rock Lighthouse is situated about 9.2 miles south-west of Land's End and it would be to our left-hand side during the swim. It was first proposed as long ago as 1790 that a lighthouse should be built on this rogue body of rock that randomly jutted out of the sea where it was least expected. It wasn't until 1840 that a beacon was finally constructed on this rock, but only four months after completion, it was obliterated by a storm and lost to the sea. Two years later the beacon was rebuilt, and this time it lasted two years before again being taken victim by a storm. It became very clear that this outcrop of rock was not only a very dangerous hazard for seafarers, but it was also a very treacherous place to attempt any kind of construction. Yet another beacon was erected on the rock which took an amazing five years to build and was completed in 1848. Twelve years later, money was provided to construct a masonry lighthouse which would stand at a massive thirty-six metres in height. This structure would go on to house the very latest optic technology with a lantern that used curved rather than straight panes of glass that had been exhibited at the Paris Exhibition of 1867.

Over the coming decades, many alterations and improvements were made to this lighthouse, including the introduction of electricity in 1955, which would replace oil burners and clockwork mechanisms. However, in 1972 Wolf Rock Lighthouse became renowned for being the first lighthouse in the world with a helipad built on top. This would make it easier and safer to transport the lighthouse keepers to and from the rock. I couldn't help thinking how wonderful it was that our relay team were hoping to achieve a world-first swim across this stretch of water, and in doing so, we would be passing a lighthouse that had also achieved its own world first.

As we made our way to the Isles of Scilly there would be another seamark over to our right, whose purpose was also to warn seafarers of imminent danger; this was not a lighthouse but a lightship. The Sevenstones Lightship is there to guide boats away from the Seven Stones Reef, which has totalled up an estimated 200 shipwrecks over the centuries. The original lightship was moored here in 1841 but, due to its exposed location and being subjected to the fiercest North Atlantic storms, it has naturally been replaced many times. In 1987, the Sevenstones Lightship became fully automated and, as a result, there was no longer a need for anyone to have to work in this desolate and vulnerable location.

During our crossing, we could expect to see other sea vessels on their various journeys and crossing our paths from all directions. Then there would be the magnificent wildlife. It is always a wonderful sight when a fish passes by underneath you while swimming in the sea. I hoped we would see plenty of fish. What I was also hoping for was to see lots of jellyfish. Although I appreciate that jellyfish are not always a welcome sight for some swimmers, including a couple on our team, I personally find it very relaxing to watch them gently propel themselves through the water with such grace and elegance. I also don't mind coming into contact with them as long as they don't sting, which I have experienced a number of times. The only time I remember being quite freaked out by jellyfish was an incident that happened a few years previously when I went for a swim in the river Stour. This river was very wide at the point where I was swimming, and once I was about half a mile out from the bank, I encountered a deluge of jellyfish like you could never imagine. There were so many of them that I was no longer swimming through water, I was pulling my way through jelly! They were all over me, and my face was simply pushing its way into a thick wall of jelly. As much as I wasn't enjoying this experience, I was just thankful that they were not stingers. It only took me a matter of seconds to realize this was the case and I was so relieved. If they had been stingers, and given the amount I encountered, I doubt I would still be here to tell the tale. Despite this, I still love encountering jellyfish.

We didn't anticipate seeing a walrus on our swim, now that Wally had decided to return to his homeland. However, there would certainly be the possibility of seeing some dolphins on our journey, which would be a wonderful sight. But on the flip side there was also a chance of encountering sharks.

It was just a few days before we were due to head down to Penzance when I had a chat to Cathy. She told me she had just been on the phone to our pilot Mark to talk about our arrangements and he just happened to mention to Cathy that he was out with a group of tourists, shark spotting! This was something I really didn't need to hear just a few days before we were due to swim in that very same stretch of water. Although I had previously undergone hypnotherapy for a fear of sharks prior to my solo Channel swim, this news was still not something that was going to fill me with a great deal of confidence. I swear that Cathy gets a huge amount of pleasure from winding me up.

The day before I was due to head down to Brighton for my marathon, I had a lot to organize. Richard had kindly offered to take my suitcase and swim bag down in the car with them, so I didn't have so much luggage to carry on my train journey to Penzance. I would then just have my rucksack to take with me. I also had to sort out an overnight bag to take to Brighton, as well as making sure I had all my running gear and nutrition prepared for my marathon.

Late that morning I drove over to Richard's workplace to drop my luggage off with him. We had a quick chat and we were both very much looking forward to our big swim the following week. I then headed off to Asda for food shopping and then back home for lunch. Just as everything appeared to be running smoothly and as planned, I received a message from Sam that stopped me dead in my tracks! I scanned the message a second time just to make sure I hadn't misread it in any way. It said:

'I think it is highly unlikely this swim will happen. I've just been talking to a skipper I work with who's heading back from Scotland to arrive on Wednesday ahead of the huge low pressure coming in on the Atlantic which is the storm from America.'

I had been all too aware of this storm in America and knew at some point it would head our way, but I, just hoped it wouldn't be quite yet. Now Sam had been given information that this storm could be arriving on the Wednesday. That was the very day our swim window began. If this was the case then there would be no chance of us even starting our swim, let alone completing it!

I was absolutely gutted. So much had been invested into this swim in terms of training, organization, finances and of course commitment. How could it just be taken away from us like this? Obviously, we were all well aware that this is the nature of open-water swimming, but in my head, it was all going to work out perfectly. I had visualized us landing successfully in the Scilly Isles more times than I could remember and I thought that would definitely be the case. Now this whole dream of mine was being totally blown out of the water by an approaching storm.

Almost immediately, I entered into a state of denial. Surely this information must be wrong? This storm can't be arriving on Wednesday? I sent a very simple message back to Sam saying that we must stay positive and hope for the best. Sam told me she had already spoken to Cathy and so I called Cathy immediately.

While on the phone to Cathy, she did sound rather down about the whole situation and that was totally understandable. We obviously had the discussion about whether we should all still travel down to Cornwall in the hope that the storm was a little delayed and conditions may possibly allow us to attempt our swim. I was totally up for this and Cathy agreed and said she would speak to the others to get their views.

It was soon fed back to me that everyone was in agreement that we should continue with our plans to head down to Penzance in preparation for the swim just in case conditions did work out alright for us. I had already put my argument across that if we travelled down and then the swim was called off due to the weather, that would be a much easier situation to deal with than deciding to not head down and then discovering that we could have actually had a crack at it.

That evening, as I packed the last few items for my Brighton Marathon weekend, I couldn't help feeling rather empty and sad inside. In the next few days, I was not only going to attempt my 'comeback' marathon with inadequate training and a leg still recovering from surgery, but then I was hoping to achieve a world-first relay swim to the Isles of Scilly with a great bunch of people. However, this swim may very well not happen due to the weather. What if I didn't complete one of these two challenges? How would I feel about that? Obviously, out of the two I would much rather achieve our relay swim. But I couldn't help wondering what impact it would have on me if neither of these events were successful. How would I cope with that mentally? Would I feel like a failure? I couldn't really predict how I would feel if I achieved neither of these goals, but what I did know was that if I had given everything I had for both of these challenges then it would certainly ease the pain if the outcome for one or both was not desirable. Emphasis should always be put on the process rather than the desired outcome.

Getting to sleep that night was a tricky task with everything zooming about in my mind. In fact, it was probably mental exhaustion that finally took me under and gave me a little respite before my alarm went off a few hours later, initiating the start of one of the most challenging weeks of my life so far.

Information for this chapter sourced from:

- https://www.trinityhouse.co.uk/lighthouses-and-lightvessels/ wolf-rock-lighthouse
- https://www.trinityhouse.co.uk/lighthouses-and-lightvessels/ sevenstones-lightvessel

SEVEN

THE BRIGHTON MARATHON WEEKEND

At around 10am Cherie and I started our journey down to Brighton so I could register and pick my race number up for my marathon the following day. We decided to use the park and ride and arrived at the expo village, which was situated on the beach, around midday.

I felt like a bit of a fraud when I picked my race number up because I had put myself down for the wave of runners that were expecting to finish in around 3:30:00. My fastest marathon to date was 3:59:42 and I was nowhere near as prepared this time and was expecting around five hours. The problem was, I had not read the instructions properly when I booked the park and ride for the marathon. After I had booked it Cherie then read that I had to move the car by 16:30 or it would be towed away! I couldn't believe I had been so stupid. So, if I went in my correct wave I would be starting about an hour later, giving me just six hours to complete the marathon, get out of the finishing area, walk to the bus stop and have a twenty- to thirty-minute journey to the park and ride. This would be really cutting it fine and there would be very little margin for any unforeseen circumstances. So, my only option was to go in a much faster wave and hope I didn't get trampled underfoot at the start.

Having booked myself in without any drama, I stood there with my goodie bag in hand and feeling very pleased with myself that my devious plan was working. We only had a short wait for the return bus back to the park and ride. The bus was quite full, but as we slowly made our way along the seafront, it stopped regularly and the number of passengers began to dwindle. I recognized the route we were taking as I had run along it as part of my first Brighton Marathon and it would also be the route I would take the following day. We also realised that we were heading in the opposite direction to the park and ride so naturally assumed that the bus was doing a large circuit and we would soon be heading back. The bus took us out into the countryside and we had some stunning views out to sea as we were high up on the cliffs. By now there were just two or three other passengers on board. Eventually, we came to a village and the bus stopped again. The remainder of the passengers exited the bus and we sat there alone.

Then the bus driver noticed us, turned around and said, "This is the end of the line."

I explained to him that we were heading for the park and ride and this was the number bus we were told to catch. He seemed rather amused as he explained that we were indeed on the right number bus but that we should have caught the bus on the other side of the road; the one heading in the opposite direction. I felt such a fool! Luckily, he explained that we would only have a short wait before we started heading back that way.

Before long we were travelling back along the clifftop and the bus began to refill with passengers. Then at one stop the driver got off and was replaced by another. I felt slightly relieved that there was no longer anybody present on the bus that was witness to our accidental marathon journey back to the park and ride.

Eventually we passed the expo where we had begun this journey and finally started making some actual progress towards our destination. However, we were only a couple of miles from the park and ride when the bus pulled over. The driver got up and announced that the bus had broken down. So, we had to change onto another bus for the remainder of the journey.

Finally, we arrived at the park and ride. A journey which should have taken twenty minutes had turned out to be a lengthy hour-and-a-half ride, not to mention the two buses and three different drivers!

I was so relieved to get back into my car knowing we just had a short trip to Worthing where we had a hotel room waiting for us. I started to drive out of the car park and became aware of a strange noise. A loud rattling noise. Cherie asked what it was and I said it may not be the car, it could be something else. I stopped and turned the engine off and the noise was no longer there. Oh bugger! Instinctively, I had a feeling it was the exhaust pipe making the noise. I checked underneath the car in case there was something hanging off but I couldn't see anything obvious. We had no choice but to just get on with our journey and hope for the best.

As we rattled our way to Worthing, I couldn't help thinking what a coincidence it was that the car was having problems with the exhaust and that the last time I attempted to run a marathon at Hockley Woods in Essex back in March 2017 we also had an issue with our exhaust pipe just before the run.

On that occasion Cherie and I were driving down the A12 and were a few miles from our destination when there was a loud 'clunk' followed by a very loud scraping sound. Cars started flashing me, so I pulled over to discover the exhaust pipe had come apart and was dragging on the road, probably causing sparks. I suppose the sensible thing to do in this situation would have been to call for recovery, but as we were now so close to the start point of our marathon, I decided I would drive slowly and cautiously so that we didn't miss out on the event.

When we arrived at the car park, I called the recovery service and explained what the problem was. The lady on the other end of the phone told me that it was unlikely that the problem could be rectified on the roadside and so would probably need a recovery truck to take us and our car back home. I assumed this would be the case. She then said she could probably get someone to me within two hours. I felt a little silly while verbalizing my response to her. "Could you not send them for about six hours if that's OK?"

After a slight pause she replied, "Err OK that's fine. Do you mind me asking why you want to wait longer than you have to?"

"I've gotta run a marathon before being picked up," I said.

The lady on the phone laughed and said she had never received a request like that before but also said it was fine and wished me good luck.

Unfortunately, on this occasion the luck this lady wished me was simply not enough as this was the first marathon I did not complete. Without trying to make excuses, my head simply wasn't in running mode that day. I had experienced a particularly stressful situation at work just a few days previously and this was still playing on my mind. Add to that the issue I was having with the car. The course itself was tough and I ran the majority of it alone and much of it in shoe-sucking, energy-draining mud. It was also a lap event and a medal was given to anyone completing at least one lap. I had to run eight laps to complete my fourteenth marathon. With it being laps, it means you are also having to run past a finish line to begin the next lap. After completing each lap, you had the option of pulling out and still receiving a medal. Obviously, I wasn't doing this for a medal, I simply wanted to complete another marathon, but on this occasion, I felt mentally broken, and after five laps (16.5 miles), I pulled out feeling extremely disappointed with myself.

So, this Brighton Marathon was my comeback run I suppose. It was the opportunity for me to prove to myself that I was still able to complete the distance. However, having this problem with the exhaust again, I couldn't help feeling this was a bad omen. Maybe this was going to be history repeating itself? What were the chances of me having car exhaust issues on two consecutive marathons? I had to try and push that thought out of my head as well as all the other negative intrusive scenarios that were playing in my mind and trying their best to bring me down and make me fail. I had to stay positive.

We booked into our hotel, and after a shower and a quick nap, it was time to meet up with our daughter Phoebe, her boyfriend at the time Chris and his mother Clare. Chris lived with his mother in Worthing and Phoebe was staying with them, so it was an ideal opportunity for us all to have a meal together, and then the following day they wanted to come along to cheer me on and of course the thousands of other runners who were competing in the Brighton Marathon.

All that was left now were some last-minute preparations, such as pinning my run number to my top and making sure I had everything I needed in my pouch. Then I just needed to sleep before an early start in the morning.

I always find it difficult to switch off and sleep before a big event. I lay there with my eyes closed mulling things over in my mind. Would I still be able to complete a marathon so soon after my varicose vein operation and the inevitable disruption to my training schedule? Would my knees behave themselves? This was always a concern for me in any running event. Then I was worried about the car. Would my exhaust fall off on the way to the park and ride? Then of course would it get me back home afterwards? If I didn't get home that evening, how would I make it to the train the following morning to begin my journey down to Penzance? Not to mention the time restraint I had to complete the marathon and get back to the park and ride before having the car towed away. There were so many different variables that could happen to prevent me from either completing the marathon or getting back home that evening or both!

Somehow, I must have eventually drifted off to sleep because suddenly the alarm was going off and it was time to get up. After checking out of the hotel, we took the short walk to where the car was parked. I was as nervous about the car getting us there as I was about the marathon itself. I started it up and it didn't sound great. We just had to get on with it and hope for the best.

Thankfully, we got to the park and ride safely and were soon on the bus that was taking us to the start area at Preston Park. Once we arrived, I made a final check that I had everything I needed. I had brought a fleece with me that I could discard at the start of the race, but the sun was already quite warm so I didn't even need to wear it. Cherie wished me good luck and then I made my way into the park where thousands of other runners were already gathered and awaiting the start.

Eventually, it was time to join the huge queue of runners, and as we were slowly shepherded into position for the start, I noticed a message on my phone from my friend Danielle at work. This surprised me as Danielle is notorious for not replying to messages and very rarely sends the first one. I wondered if it was something important, but no, it was just a casual enquiry as to how I was doing. As I shuffled forwards in the crowd towards the start line, I sent a quick reply saying that I was just about to start, Brighton Marathon. She had forgotten I was running that day but it did make me laugh that on the very rare occasion Danielle decided to send me a random message, she chose that moment.

At 09:30am the race began, and as I crossed the start line, I started my stopwatch and had to remind myself that I was amongst much faster runners than me and must be mindful to not get swept along with them at a pace I could not sustain. Despite keeping this in mind, I still managed to complete the first couple of miles quicker than I had planned to.

The sun was already very warm and the temperature was set to continue to rise over the duration of the marathon. I had only just passed the four-mile marker when I had sudden pain in my right knee. I'm used to pains and twinges in my knees while running so I just continued in the hope that it would quickly pass. However, a couple of minutes later, it was still very uncomfortable, so I stopped to give it some attention. I was now very concerned that I may have to pull out at a very early stage. After a short rest and some gentle movement, I started running again and it was feeling a lot better, but I still had this uneasy feeling that it would return and I wasn't even a fifth of the way around the course yet.

As predicted, the pain in my knee returned a couple more times before the halfway mark, requiring me to stop briefly. Despite this, I was still on for a reasonable time. Just before reaching halfway, I saw some frantic waving up ahead. It was Cherie, Phoebe, Chris and Clare cheering me on. I stopped for a very quick chat and explained about my knee. Then, after swapping my drink bottle for a fresh one, I was once again on my way, pleased with my time so far but still concerned about my knee being able to support me for another thirteen miles.

The heat became much more intense now and I was aware I was taking on a huge amount of fluid as well as tipping plenty over my head in an attempt to cool down. A few of the feed stations even had cold water showers to run under. I have to admit I did slow down considerably while passing under the showers as it just felt so good.

At around mile eighteen, my knee became very painful again. This was so frustrating. I stopped and gently moved it about, but the pain didn't want to go. So, I continued running, and after a while, it did ease a bit.

However, just as I was passing the twenty-mile marker, the pain returned with a vengeance. This time there was no way I could even attempt to run on it. I was gutted, but there was no chance I was going to quit. The only thing I could do was to limp on in the vague hope that things would improve and allow me to continue running.

This was a part of the course with relatively few spectators, and I was glad of that. Over the next two miles, I had a couple of attempts to break out into a jog, but they were very short-lived as the pain was just too much. I had now resigned myself to the fact that I was going to have to limp my way for the four miles that remained. Any hope of anything that remotely resembled a half-decent time was now well and truly out of the window. My only aim now was to make it to the finish line.

I thought about the last time I had gone past this section during my very first marathon back in 2014 and how I was increasing my pace as the possibility of a sub four-hour marathon became more and more of a reality. It was around here that I was also cheered on by Zoe Ball and Fat Boy Slim, but there was no sign of either of them on this occasion.

As I limped my way down the never-ending promenade, the number of spectators began to grow. People were cheering me on and encouraging me to run, but obviously they didn't understand that I hadn't stopped running because I was worn out I simply couldn't run due to being injured.

Then a smartly dressed young man approached me and asked if he could help as he could see I was in pain. He wondered if I had cramp but I explained it was my knee that was the problem. He again said that he wanted to help, and although I had no idea what he could do right there and then to improve things for me, I was happy to accept anything that was on offer. The man placed a hand on my shoulder and his other hand on my injured knee. He then began a monologue of what I believe were passages from the Bible. I stood there for a minute or so while he performed his healing on me. When he finished, I thanked him and he wished me well.

There was obviously only one way to find out if my knee was now miraculously cured and that was to start running on it again. So that is exactly what I did and, to my surprise and relief, I did not experience any pain. Well at least not for the next minute or so, but then it returned as bad as it was before and I again had to resort to limping. Did I think the man was a fraud? Absolutely not! Maybe if he had asked me for money for his services then that would be a different matter entirely. But clearly this man's intentions were good and noble and that's all that should really matter. Had I been naïve in thinking he could heal me? I know many people would say I had been, but I already had personal experience of a miracle cure on a long-standing shoulder injury following my solo English Channel swim. After hearing a mysterious voice while lying on a soggy boat on the way back to England, I was suddenly healed of my injury that had plagued me for many months. So, I knew these things were certainly possible. Maybe the young man just needed more practice or was just having an 'off day'. Whatever the case, it was a kind gesture by a complete stranger and that was very much appreciated.

As I saw the pier gradually getting closer, I knew my ordeal was almost over as the finish line was just beyond it. Apart from the obvious pain in my knee and a severe thirst, I felt quite good physically. Having been reduced to walking speed for the last few miles meant I had not expended as much energy as I would have expected to. Energy wise I was easily able to be running at this point but injury was preventing me from doing so. I felt somewhat cheated and I was also disappointed that it had turned out this way. I just wanted to run another marathon without any dramas. I hadn't been hoping to complete it in a good time but I was expecting it to be around the five-hour mark. Now I knew it was going to be more like six hours. I wanted to try and process all this negativity and come to terms with the situation before I reached the finish, so as to hopefully enjoy a little bit of glory when I crossed the line.

As I got closer to the finish, the crowds grew even larger and the noise from the cheering and clapping was very loud. I knew Cherie and the others would be somewhere around the finish but somehow I missed them. I was later informed that I limped right past them as they shouted out my name but I was somehow oblivious to their presence. They even showed me photos they had taken, which included evidence of a female runner tapping me on the shoulder and pointing towards my group of supporters and yet I simply plodded on in my own little world.

As I came round the last bend, the end was in sight. There was no way I was going to limp over the finish line as I had never finished a marathon walking before, so I gritted my teeth and broke out into a jog. The pain in my knee was excruciating but I only had about 200m to go. I just had to get on with it. Finally, I crossed the line and hobbled over to collect my medal.

I was still somewhat disappointed that my knee had let me down, but at the same time, I was happy that I had completed another marathon after my previous non-finish. Marathon number fourteen was finally in the bag.

Proudly holding my medal on Brighton beach.

I slowly made my way out of the finishing area and along the promenade a little further to where I had agreed to meet back up with the others. Congratulations were given and I felt I needed to explain my knee issue to them and why it had taken me so long to complete it. In turn they told me about the frustrating moment when I passed them by while they were screaming my name but I was oblivious to their presence. There was only time to take a few quick photos of me on the beach with my new medal before Cherie and I had to walk up an agonizingly steep road to catch the last bus back to our car at the park and ride.

My official time was 6:04:52 which was my slowest marathon by far. It was over half an hour slower than my Beachy Head marathon, which was a very challenging trail course. However, it soon came to light that there had been a miscalculation in the measuring of the Brighton Marathon that year. The course had been slightly altered from the one used in previous years and someone, or some people, had made an error. Apparently, it was remeasured, and instead of running the standard 26.2 miles, we had in fact run a further 568 meters. I did joke that I had technically just completed an ultra-marathon, but it also meant that, because of the very slow pace I was moving at, when I reached the 26.2-mile point, I would have still been under six hours. Just the fact that I knew I had reached marathon distance in five hours and something made me feel much better about my achievement.

The drive home to Bury St Edmunds was not a comfortable journey to say the least. Firstly, my knee was still very painful. Just the movement of using the accelerator and brake pedals was enough to cause more than a little discomfort. Secondly, the car was still rattling and there was a constant fear that the exhaust could drop off at any moment, resulting in a certain degree of anxiety.

Luckily, we made it home safely and I couldn't wait to have a shower and relax in my favorite chair with a lovely cup of tea. When I say relax, I mean as much as I possibly could whilst having to elevate my right leg and put frozen peas on my knee to help with the pain and the now obvious swelling. Oh, and of course there was that little matter of having to take a very long train journey down to Penzance in the morning, to embark on the next part of the week, attempting a world-first relay swim from mainland Britain to the Isles of Scilly. I didn't want to think too much about this next challenge at that moment, and luckily, Phoebe and Chris arrived home soon after us and my mind was distracted for a while as we recollected the comical moments of the weekend.

Before long, the evening was over and I slowly hobbled up the stairs to bed. As I lay there in the dark, my thoughts once again went into overdrive. Thoughts about the marathon that day and thoughts about what may lie in the week ahead. I had succeeded in completing my marathon but I was injured. Obviously, I had known all along that this was a possibility, but I also knew this would not affect my ability to swim. If I had been considering participating in an event that could have resulted in a shoulder injury, then I would never have gone ahead with it. I had an injured knee, but my arms and shoulders were fine and I was happy with that. All I wanted was my thoughts to stop racing around in my head as I needed some well-earned and much-needed sleep.

EIGHT

PENZANCE

As I slowly emerged from my state of slumber, I felt good. My legs were aching a lot, but it was that lovely post-marathon pain that I enjoyed so much. A pain that may be uncomfortable but makes up for it by reminding you of a great achievement. It was my happy pain, and I felt contented and relaxed.

Then, all of a sudden, my brain also woke up. My moment of euphoria was over as I remembered I had a train to catch to get me down to Penzance for the start of our relay swim. A swim I then remembered may well not even go ahead because of a storm coming over from America. I then remembered it was also Cherie's birthday and there was limited time to give my wife her card and present before rushing off to the train station.

I decided I couldn't afford to waste a moment longer and so I sat on the edge of the bed and stood up. It was at that precise moment I remembered the knee injury. There were two reasons I was suddenly reminded of this. The first was the excruciating pain in my right knee as I put weight on it. The second was the fact that my right leg buckled underneath me and I found myself once again sitting on the edge of the bed. Oh bugger!

Clearly, I realized that this was not going to be an easy journey down the stairs, let alone the imminent walk to the train station, followed by four separate train journeys that would hopefully deliver me safely to Penzance that evening. I concluded that I had a long and uncomfortable day ahead of me.

After dosing myself up on pain medication, Phoebe then offered to strap my knee up to give it some support. After she had attended to my knee, I felt like there was not much more that could be done to ease the pain and so I would just have to grin and bare it.

However, my knee wasn't the only thing giving me pain, as I also discovered I had phlebitis on the back of my thigh on the same leg. I had originally spoken to the doctor about this large vein on the back of my right leg many years before, but this wasn't the vein they decided to perform the ablation on. Now it was swollen and very tender when touched. Luckily, I already had some anti-inflammatory cream to apply to it.

Normally it would take about twenty-five minutes to walk to the train station, but we decided to allow fifty, as I was not going to be walking at any great speed. Obviously, the easy option would have been to call for a taxi. However, knowing that I was going to be spending the best part of the day sitting on a train, I was worried my legs would totally seize up if I didn't get them working again. So, I decided a hobble to the station was what I needed to do. Also, since when have I ever taken the easy option? Cherie, Sean and Phoebe accompanied me on my slow trek and Sean kindly offered to carry my rucksack to reduce the weight on my injured knee.

Every step I took caused me pain, but I was hoping that walking would start to make things better. A couple of weeks previously I had made an agreement with Megan that we would both run Land's End parkrun together after our swim. As the two of us would be based only a few miles from this iconic parkrun, it seemed logical that we should run it. It was me that came up with this idea of running Land's End parkrun and suggested it to Megan, so I had to take full responsibility for it. As I limped my way to the train station, this agreement came into my mind. It was Monday and so parkrun was only five days away. Here I was, struggling to even walk, and so the very thought of running was completely unfathomable to me. I decided Land's End parkrun was almost definitely out of the question, although my running gear was already in Penzance with the rest of my luggage, so there would always be that temptation.

We made it to the train station in good time and I took a photo of the 'Bury St Edmunds' sign on the wall and sent it to our group chat. I decided I would send pictures of the various train stations on my journey so the others could track my progress towards them down in Penzance.

Soon the train arrived and I said my farewells to the family as they all wished me good luck. As the train pulled out of the station and I sat there alone, the reality of our relay swim suddenly struck me more than ever before. I had thought about the swim so much over the previous couple of years, but now I was actually on the train and starting my journey down to Penzance where the actual adventure would begin, and it filled me with excitement. However, at the back of my mind was that nagging thought about the inevitable arrival of the storm coming across the Atlantic. It was now a matter of timing, and all we could do was hope Neptune would give us the chance to attempt our swim.

In no time at all the train pulled up at Stowmarket station where I had to catch my connection to Liverpool Street in London. By a strange coincidence, my sister-in-law Amber had been visiting us in Bury St Edmunds and was travelling back home to Bristol the same day. However, Amber had booked a different train to me and was taking the alternative route via Cambridge. As we were both arriving in London around the same time, Amber had agreed to meet me at Liverpool Street station where we took the tube to Paddington. Here we had about an hour to kill before we boarded our respective trains around the same time. Amber's train was heading for Bristol while mine would take me on the five-and-a-half-hour, final part of my journey to Penzance.

I found my way to my pre-booked window seat, only to find a young woman already occupying it. The carriage was filling up fast and there were not many seats left. I thought about informing her that she was sitting in my seat but decided to say nothing and to just sit next to her in the hope that I wasn't taking anyone else's pre-booked seat. Then an announcement came over the loudspeaker saying that five carriages had been removed from the train and therefore all pre-booked seats had been scrapped. Maybe the young woman already knew this, and I was just relieved that I hadn't confronted her about it as that could have been awkward. I was also glad that I had a seat at all because it soon became clear that many people would have to stand for their journey. I'm not sure how I would have coped if I was forced to stand on a moving train with my dodgy knee.

As we rolled gently out of Paddington station it was hot and stuffy, and the train was far too crowded for comfort. I figured that it wouldn't be like that for the whole journey as passengers would disembark along the route and hopefully fewer would join us. Luckily, I was right, and after about an hour, there were even empty seats in the carriage. A while later we pulled up at a station and the woman in my seat asked politely if I could let her out. What a relief, I finally had my window seat, and even a spare one next to me for my rucksack. As may have become clear, I'm not a regular train traveller.

As I was enjoying the ever-changing view out of the window, I overheard a conversation that was happening from a few seats behind me. A man was telling his fellow passenger that his legs were very sore and stiff as he had run the Brighton Marathon the day before. This amused me greatly and I wished I could join in with their chat, but it just wasn't practical. It may have been a much more enjoyable journey if this man had been seated next to me so we could have had a conversation about a shared experience.

Once we started to glide our way through the Somerset countryside, I knew I was well on my way to Penzance. I was now so grateful to have my window seat back so that I could appreciate the views. Before long, we entered Devon with its beautiful rolling hills of deep red soil. The Devon landscape always looks so rich and fertile and almost like you could eat it.

Finally, we entered Cornwall, and by now, the carriage had only a handful of passengers left. Also, the weather had taken a turn for the worse. I had left Bury St Edmunds in lovely bright sunshine which had remained for most of the journey, but now it was grey and raining.

The train passed through some very familiar places, as we had been on several family holidays in Cornwall. Stopping at St Austell station brought back memories of staying here briefly when Cherie was running the Eden Project Marathon several years previously. I was only there as a spectator on that occasion as this was before I had ever run a marathon myself, and yet the previous day I had just completed my fourteenth marathon, with emphasis on 'just'!

Pulling up at Hayle station evoked some wonderful memories of our last family holiday, which was also one of my favourites. Coincidentally, it was also where Phoebe and Chris had been away together the previous week, so I took a picture of the sign and sent it to Phoebe.

I was tracking my progress on my phone and eventually I could see that we were approaching Penzance. I simply couldn't wait to meet up with the team and start talking about swimming. I felt that too much of my focus had been on running over the weekend, but I knew once I was in the house with the team then it would all be about swimming, and that's what I both wanted and needed.

As we approached Penzance station it was absolutely pouring with rain outside. I was entering a new part of our country and also a completely different climate to the one I had left that morning. I also needed to use the toilet quite desperately but knew there would be facilities at the station. The train finally came to a halt at its final destination, and it was time to get up and walk again after several hours of being seated. I was relieved that I didn't have to struggle my way down the aisle holding people up who were eager to get home, because luckily by now there was only one other person on our carriage, who had been sitting at the window seat opposite me for the whole journey. As we emerged from our seats, I felt like I should congratulate her on surviving the journey but then quickly realized, as she sprung out of her seat and rushed for the door, that it was only me that had suffered with painful and aching legs on this long train ride. Now I had to struggle to walk again following this long period of inactivity. My knee was just as painful and now my leg muscles were also seizing up.

As I limped my way down the platform, I was eagerly looking for a sign telling me where the toilet was. I spotted one and headed in that direction, but once I got there, I discovered it to be locked. There was a notice on the door informing me of its opening times. Clearly my train had arrived too late for me to be able to appreciate all the facilities this train station had to offer at other times of the day.

I exited the train station in the pouring rain and realized I was right next to the sea. Then I stopped for a moment and looked around me, taking in all the sights, sounds and smells, and felt a huge amount of joy. I was so happy that everything had gone to plan up until this moment and also thrilled to be back in Cornwall.

Using my phone to try and navigate myself to the holiday house proved to be quite problematic in the heavy rain, not to mention that I had very little signal and so attempts to text or call my teammates kept failing. Oh, and did I mention I really needed to use the toilet? Luckily, en route I came across a Weatherspoons pub. As soon as I saw it, all I could think of was having use of a toilet and being in the dry so I could use my phone. This was also the same Weatherspoons pub that Cherie and I and the kids had been to several years previously on our last family holiday. As I walked through the doors, it brought back some happy times and I even remembered the table we all sat at for our meal. I then hobbled up the stairs to the toilet before returning a very relieved man.

Now that I was in this dry safe haven, I decided I should take stock of the situation and plan where I needed to go next. Obviously, I couldn't take advantage of the facilities I had at hand without giving something back, and so I ordered a pint and sat down at a table to plan my next move. After a few exchanges of messages, I was sure I knew where I had to go, and it was where I was originally heading in the first place.

After finishing my pint, and with a new-found determination to reach the others, I ventured back out into the deluge of rain. I was already soaked through, and every second that passed, it just got worse. After all, I was only wearing a hoodie because when I left sunny Suffolk that morning, I had no idea that I would be faced with these kinds of conditions.

Finally, I entered the road where our house was. All I had to do was simply walk the length of the street looking at every house name until I found my home for the next week. I had even been sent a picture earlier on with George standing at the front door so I also had a visual clue to help me, although I guessed that George wouldn't still be standing there.

I slowly walked down one side of the road, carefully inspecting the house names with no positive result. *Great*, I thought, *but at least I've narrowed it down to the other side.* After slowly limping my way back up the road and finding nothing that even resembled our house, I felt totally broken.

It was still pouring with rain and I couldn't get any wetter than if I was actually swimming in the sea. I looked back down the long, dark street, thinking, *those buggers are down there somewhere!* I kept trying to call Richard for help but the signal repeatedly cut out. At least he knew I was having problems finding them. I had even managed to get a text message through to Cherie to inform her of my situation, just in case the worst happened and I was found dead at the side of the road the following morning. I'm sure she really appreciated that information while trying to enjoy her birthday.

I had no choice but to head back down that damn road and start my search all over again. As I ploughed on into the torrential rain, I noticed a dark silhouette trudging its way up the pavement towards me. I felt excited just to see another human being, let alone someone that may be able to help me find my destination. As this person got closer, I could see that it was a woman and she looked a bit flustered. We both stopped and greeted each other. I was just about to ask her for some directions, assuming she was a local and would know exactly where I needed to go, but before I could even open my mouth, she asked me for directions to a local guest house.

Obviously, I hadn't got a clue where this young woman was heading for. I couldn't help but laugh, and I had no delight when informing her that I was as lost as she was. Looking at each other with rain dripping off our noses, I think we both found the funny side of the situation. We wished each other good luck and headed off in opposite directions. As I made my way once again back down this road, I couldn't help thinking that it was pointless because I had already thoroughly checked every property on both sides and had got nowhere.

I tried checking my phone again in the pouring rain and noticed a message from Richard saying that he would come out and try to look for me. I was so grateful of this as I was already having disturbing thoughts of spending the night sleeping on the street somewhere. How do you sleep on the street in the pouring rain? The fact is thousands of people have to do this every night. I don't know how they do it and I have every respect for the fact that they do and somehow manage to survive. There I was feeling sorry for myself because I was lost in an unfamiliar place and was soaking wet, and yet I knew somehow that I would eventually make it to my friends and have a hot meal and a comfortable bed to sleep in.

I thought I was somewhat hardcore because I had previously swum across the English Channel, completed a 100-mile ultra run and was now about to take on a world-first relay attempt to the Isles of Scilly. Yet I couldn't bear the thought of sleeping rough for the night in the pouring rain. It suddenly made me put everything into perspective. Maybe I was hardcore in some ways, but if I was, then these people who have to sleep on the street night after night are, without doubt, much tougher than me. Maybe it is these strong and resilient individuals that should be writing a book about the horrendous challenges of living life on the streets. I felt very humbled.

All of a sudden, and as if by magic, Richard appeared in front of me. I have known Richard since we were children, but I have to say this was the moment that I had never felt more pleased to see him. Finally, I would be reunited with the rest of the team and get warm and dry. When I say reunited, I was still yet to meet our team member Megan and obviously Sam would not be there, but it was as much of the team as I could hope for.

Richard and I greeted each other and then I believe there was a certain amount of 'piss-taking' by Richard because of the predicament I had found myself in. I simply had to take it on the chin. Apparently, I had not followed their directions properly and so I had nobody else to blame but myself. The house we were staying in was actually on a side road just off the road I had diligently been searching.

It was such a relief to finally be walking up the steps into the house that we were all sharing for the coming week. Cathy was the first to greet me with a big hug, and it was so welcoming. It felt great after such a long day to actually truly be there with everyone.

I was so pleased to finally meet Megan. It seemed strange to me that I was only just meeting her for the first time, only two days before we planned to embark on our relay swim. Even more astonishing was the fact that Sam and Megan would not meet until the day itself. Luckily, we had all got to know each other as best we could on our WhatsApp group, and I think we all considered that we had already bonded as a team despite not meeting in person.

I also got to meet Megan's partner Mark, who turned out to be a great support to the team, especially in the cooking department. Megan and Mark's son Owen was already fast asleep in bed so I would have to wait until the morning to finally get to meet this amazing little person.

After all the soggy greetings, I simply had to get out of my soaking wet clothes and into something dryer. I was sharing an attic room with Richard and George and so I spent the next five minutes or so heaving my way up an endless number of steps feeling pain in my knee on each one. They seemed to go on forever, but eventually I reached the summit and was pleasantly surprised at what a lovely room we were staying in for the coming week.

I hung my sopping clothes up to dry once I'd changed and was gradually beginning to feel human again. Then I had to face the long descent, which took another five minutes or so. When I finally reached the ground floor, I was handed a beer and guided into the dining room where a meal had been prepared. I had told the others not to wait for me and to have their meal without me. I would have been more than happy with leftovers. But in true team spirit they did wait for me so that we could all eat together. I was very touched by this.

Following our delicious meal, we all chatted for a while, but to be honest, I was desperate for bed and to have some decent sleep. The previous day I had completed the Brighton Marathon, and now I felt like I had just completed another marathon on my journey down to Penzance to meet up with my teammates. I was simply exhausted.

Getting to sleep that night wasn't as straightforward as I had hoped for. Sharing a room with Richard and George, and all having had a couple of pints of beer, and maybe a sneaky whisky, which I feel I must point out was actually forced upon me, meant that there was far too much talking and laughter for there to be any chance of sleep. Obviously, I'm not blaming Richard and George for keeping me awake because I am well aware that I am terrible once I start laughing. Sometimes I simply can't stop. It reminded me of the last night we all spent together in a guest house in Dover, the night before our English Channel relay swim. I have to confess that it was definitely me that was the disruption that night due to my hysterical and uncontrollable laughter!

Eventually, tiredness gradually put the brakes on the banter, and after a while, we all settled down into a deep sleep where our physical bodies could rest, but I'm sure our subconscious minds were still hard at work trying to prepare us for the monumental swim ahead.

NINE

THE DAY BEFORE

I awoke the following morning feeling chilly and windswept. A cold breeze was blowing over me, and as I tried to make sense of my surroundings there was a loud flapping and banging sound to my left. As my eyes focused some more, I realized the very large window next to my bed had somehow blown wide open during the night and the wind was causing havoc and bashing the blind around ,which had already sent several items flying onto the floor that I had placed on the windowsill the previous night. I reached up and pulled the window closed and made a mental note to be cautious of leaving the window open more than a fraction in future. Then I suddenly remembered the vicious storm that was on its way from America. The very storm that threatened to put a stop to any plans of us attempting our swim to the Isles of Scilly. I began to worry that the storm had arrived early and our plans of even starting our swim had been scuppered.

George and Richard were already awake and in the middle of a conversation. Once they realized I had finally emerged from my much-needed sleep, we then all chatted for some time while contemplating actually getting out of bed. I didn't mention to them that I feared the Atlantic storm was just outside. I preferred to pretend that there was no wind howling in the garden and that it would soon blow over.

We knew we would have a chilled and relaxed day ahead of us, but we also knew that the following day would present itself as the complete polar opposite, because that was the day that our relay swim was planned to go ahead. All going well, we would literally be heading out to sea and swimming into the unknown, without any real understanding of what we may face. It was a very daunting and yet exciting thought.

Following breakfast, we made our way to Penlee Lifeboat Station in Newlyn, just down the road from where we were staying in Penzance. We had arranged to meet up with Coxswain Patch Harvey and some of the other crew for a chat and a tour of the lifeboat. The only member of our team that wouldn't be joining us was Sam, but as she used to be a member of the Dover lifeboat crew herself, I don't think she would have missed out on much. For me, this was a totally new and exciting experience. I absolutely loved being shown around the lifeboat and chatting to the crew. It left me feeling very humbled by the duty that these amazing volunteers do for their fellow citizens.

This particular lifeboat station had unfortunately experienced a very tragic event, which happened on the 19th December 1981. At 6pm Falmouth coastguard received a distress call from *Union Star,* which was on its maiden voyage from Holland to Ireland with a cargo of agricultural fertilizer. The boat's fuel system had become contaminated with water and the crew were unable to restart the engine, and with no control over the vessel, it was now being blown towards the rugged Cornish coast.

The *Union Star* was captained by Henry Morton alongside Mate James Whittaker, Engineer George Sedgwick, Crewman Anghostino Verressimo and Crewman Manuel Lopes. This crew had made a detour to Brightlingsea in Essex to pick up Henry's wife Dawn and his teenage stepdaughters Sharon and Deanne so that they could all spend Christmas together.

The first response dispatched to this incident was a *Sea King* helicopter, but *Union Star* was being thrown about so violently in the wild sea that there was fear that the ship's mast would collide with the helicopter overhead. The crew of the *Sea King* decided that it had become too dangerous to continue with this rescue mission as they could not get close enough to get a line to the deck and were forced to retreat but remained on standby.

Union Star had now drifted to just two miles off the coastline and was in grave danger. The only other option was to initiate a sea rescue, which would be a very risky mission for all involved. The lifeboat volunteers in Mousehole were all on standby as they knew they may be called upon to assist with this sea rescue. When the call came, twelve men turned up and were willing to assist in this rescue but only eight were required. *Solomon Browne* was launched from Penlee Lifeboat Station in a courageous attempt to save the lives of the eight people on *Union Star*.

In hurricane force twelve wind and eighteen-metre waves, the *Solomon Browne* struggled for half an hour to come alongside the *Union Star* but eventually the crew managed to throw lines across. The crew on the helicopter could see the fluorescent orange life jackets of the lifeboat crew as they were preparing to catch people as they jumped across to safety.

The *Solomon Browne* contacted the coastguard to inform them they had managed to get four people off the boat. With this news the helicopter returned to base, assuming the lifeboat would now be heading back to shore. However, the crew on *Solomon Browne* decided to make a final attempt to rescue the remaining four stranded people and then, suddenly, all radio contact was lost.

The coastguard attempted to make contact with the crew on *Solomon Browne* without any success, and about ten minutes later, the lights on the lifeboat could no longer be seen.

Following this news, the *Sea King* helicopter quickly refuelled and took flight again. Lifeboats from Sennen Cove, The Lizard and

St Mary's were all launched in a desperate attempt to save their colleagues but, unfortunately, their searches were unsuccessful.

At daybreak the following day, the capsized wreckage of the *Union Star* was discovered washed up on the rocks near Tater Du Lighthouse. All eight brave lifeboat volunteers of the *Solomon Browne* had tragically lost their lives while attempting to save the eight people on board this vessel. Sixteen lives lost at sea and two of them were children.

That disaster was the last time the RNLI lost an entire crew on a mission and hopefully it will be the last. Coxswain Trevelyan Richards was posthumously awarded the RNLI's gold medal for gallantry and the rest of the crew were awarded bronze medals. The Penlee Lifeboat Station was awarded a gold medal service plaque.

Lieutenant Commander Russel Smith, who was the pilot of the *Sea King* helicopter involved in the rescue mission, recounted:

'The greatest act of courage that I have ever seen, and am ever likely to see, was the penultimate courage and dedication shown by the Penlee [crew]...

'They were truly the bravest eight men I've ever seen, who were so totally dedicated to upholding the highest standards of the RNLI.'

Following this tragic disaster, an appeal was launched for the benefit of the village of Mousehole, and a massive 3 million pounds was raised. Also, on the 19th December every year since this incident, the Christmas lights in Mousehole are switched off at 8pm for an hour as a mark of respect.

Remarkably, within a day of this disaster, enough volunteers from the village of Mousehole had signed up to form a new lifeboat crew. In 1983, the Penlee Lifeboat Station was relocated to nearby Newlyn where a larger and faster Severn-class lifeboat could be accommodated. The old boathouse at Penlee Point was left as it was and a memorial garden was established next to it in 1985 to commemorate the brave crew of the *Solomon Browne*.

We were visiting the relocated Penlee station, but there were reminders of this tragic event, such as pictures on the wall of the crew that were lost that night. If anyone is ever in any doubt as to why we wanted to raise funds to support the RNLI, then I hope this account has justified our reasons. I have no doubt that we all left that lifeboat station feeling rather emotional, humbled, and totally indebted to all the amazing men and women who risk their own lives to save those of others that are in desperate need of help. Let's also not forget that this is not their job that they get paid for. They are all volunteers.

The team minus Sam, with two of the Penlee crew and little Owen.

After some lunch back at the house, we decided to go for a little afternoon dip in the sea. Richard, George and I headed to the Jubilee lido where the others would join us a little later. We went round the back of the lido to an area called Battery Rocks. Here there were some large concrete ledges where we got changed into our trunks.

It was a lovely clear blue sky, and the sun was quite intense on our bare skin. Luckily the fierce wind that had been battering my blind that morning had died right down to a gentle breeze. There were some steps leading down to the sea, but we decided not to go in straight away. While George lay on the top ledge soaking up the rays, Richard and I sat on the bottom ledge and dangled our legs into the cool water, which was almost level with where we were seated.

It wasn't long at all before the water level rose another inch and seeped over onto the ledge. Although the sea was very calm, there would be the occasional small gentle wave which would ride over the ledge and hit the concrete wall behind us, causing it to make a return journey where the cold water would slap against our backs. George found it most amusing to listen to the pair of us scream every time this happened.

A while later Richard and I decided to launch ourselves into the water. It felt great! We both swam a little way out and then trod water while we chatted and watched other people arriving to soak up the sun or venture into the sea. When we returned to George, who was still sunbathing, he took delight in informing us that our voices had carried across the smooth surface of the water and appeared to have been amplified so that everyone on the shore could hear every word that we were saying. We both had to quickly run our conversation back over in our heads to try to establish if either of us had said anything incriminating in any way. Luckily, there was nothing too bad that we could remember.

Cathy and April arrived and they both joined us in the sea along with George, who had decided it was time to cool off. Not long after, Megan and Mark turned up with Owen and Megan was also soon in the water. Apparently, they had all come for a swim at this spot the previous day while I was travelling down on the train. This was the first time I had ever seen Megan swim, and I was pleasantly relieved at what I saw. I knew I could trust Cathy when she recommended Megan to join the team.

After getting dry and changed, Richard, George and I decided to visit the Jubilee pool bar for a drink. We sat overlooking the lido and I thought about when I was last here with Cherie and the kids back in 2012. We had a great time in that pool, which is the largest art deco, seawater lido in the United Kingdom. It is also an unusual triangular shape which was apparently influenced by the shape of a seagull in flight. The pool's longest side is a staggering ninety-eight metres long, which is seven metres longer than the Jesus Green Lido where the three of us had trained in Cambridge. Unfortunately, the Jubilee lido suffered extensive damage to the terraces and changing rooms, and the floor of the pool was completely destroyed during the terrible storms in February 2014. It cost nearly three million pounds to repair the pool which reopened in May 2016. However, in 2019, Jubilee lido had some more 'improvements' made. A corner section of the pool was partitioned off by a new wall and a 410m hole was drilled into the rock below to access geothermal energy to heat this part of the pool. It became the first lido in the United Kingdom to be heated in this way. I couldn't help feeling a little sad that the lido looked different now with this new corner section. It just didn't seem right to me that such a lovely pool which, had originally opened in 1935, had been changed in this way. I suppose that's what they call 'progress'.

Next, the three of us headed to Tesco to get some food and drink for our little adventure the next day. It's never easy deciding what food to take on a long relay swim. Certain foods may seem very appetizing while you're walking around the isles of a supermarket, but will they still have the same appeal when you are miles out to sea feeling nauseous on a small boat rocking about on the waves? Thinking back to our previous relay, it was savoury food that I could stomach the best. This was also the case when I was running a marathon. I don't have a sweet tooth generally, and at times like these I feel sick just at the thought of sugary food.

The one thing I was sure I would appreciate on the boat was a lovely chicken and mushroom Pot Noodle. This had always been my favourite Pot Noodle since I was a child. When I became a vegetarian in 1993, I was totally gutted that the chicken and mushroom Pot Noodle did not display the vegetarian symbol on the container like all the other Pot Noodle varieties did. This told me very clearly, that despite all the other Pot Noodle flavours being suitable for vegetarians, this particular one obviously was not for some reason. With a sad heart I reluctantly gave up my beloved chicken and mushroom Pot Noodle for good. It was about ten years later when I was working as a paramedic that a conversation about Pot Noodles came up between me and my colleague. I have no idea why we were having this discussion, but he asked if I had ever questioned why this particular variety of Pot Noodle was not suitable for a vegetarian, given that all the others were. He suggested that I contact the company that produced them and pose the question to them. I couldn't believe I had never thought of that before. So, without any hesitation I sent an email explaining that I had given up my favourite Pot Noodle on becoming a vegetarian and asked why this particular variety was the only one in the range that was not suitable for vegetarians. I was really happy with what happened next. Not only did they respond to my email straight away, but they also informed me that the chicken and mushroom variety was also suitable for vegetarians, but for some reason they had not labelled the pot with the appropriate symbol. I simply couldn't believe it! Should I feel happy that this was the case, and I could now return to eating one of my favourite snacks, or should I feel angry that I had been cheated and prevented from enjoying this delicious treat for a large portion of my life? I emailed straight back and told them how I'd not eaten this product for years because of their mistake. They replied again with apologies and a promise that it would be added to the packaging as soon as possible. On the way home from work that day, I popped into our local Spar and purchased two chicken and mushroom Pot Noodles. That evening, I totally indulged myself and it felt like heaven. Within a few weeks, I noticed the vegetarian sign appearing on the pots, so they had kept to their word, and I felt accomplished. I often boast that my claim to fame is being responsible for the vegetarian sign on the chicken and mushroom Pot Noodle, much to the amusement of others.

The three of us stocked our baskets with more food and drink than we would ever need for a polar expedition, but it was always better to have too much rather than too little and risk running out. It also meant we had more variety to choose from to cater for our tastes at the time.

Once back at the house, it was lovely to meet Cathy's mum and dad, Liz and Ian, who had travelled down to support the team and see us off the following day. They were both full of smiles and excitement about their daughter taking on such a massive challenge. Liz and Ian joined us for our evening meal and the feeling around the table was simply electric. We were all buzzing with excitement, anticipation, and hope that everything we had been preparing for over two years would all come together and work out perfectly for us the following day.

During the meal, I had a text from Tia, which I shared with everyone. She was wishing us good luck and asking what we were having for our 'last supper'. This was a term one of us had come up with during our last meal before our English Channel relay. I can't even remember what we had on that 'last supper', but on this occasion, it was pizza. Tia had still not given birth at this point, but labour was imminent. I remember saying to the others that it would be amazing if Tia gave birth on the day we swam to the Isles of Scilly. I think we all appreciated that Tia would be enduring her own challenge very soon and definitely had a genuine excuse for missing this particular swim. I decided I would let her off!

We had a relaxing evening chatting about the swim and making final arrangements. However, there was one final hurdle we had to jump over before we were able to even attempt this relay. Something that we had no control over and in many ways, we were dreading. We all had to have a covid test, and if any one of us tested positive then the whole event would have to

Tia's excuse for not joining us on our swim.

be called off. After all we had been through over the previous couple of years with training and organizing this relay, and the personal difficulties we had to overcome, it could all have been in vain should one of us test positive. The wait for the results was agonizing but eventually we could all confirm that we were negative with Sam sending us a photo of her result, we had the final green light for our swim to go ahead.

After organizing my kit for the following day, it was finally time to try and get some decent sleep as we could not be sure how long it would be before we would next get some proper rest. There was just one final thing to do before I drifted off, and that was to make sure the window was only open a fraction, just in case we got some fierce wind during the night again.

Information for this chapter sourced from:

- https://jubileepool.co.uk/
- https://rnli.org/about-us/our-history/timeline/1981-penlee-lifeboat-disaster

TEN

JOURNEY TO
THE START

I awoke disorientated, and then as I felt a gentle breeze from the widow my nerves kicked into overdrive with worries of a storm heading our way across the Atlantic. How would our day pan out and would the relay be going ahead? At this point in time the conditions seemed fairly positive, but the weather is unpredictable and can change in an instant, especially out at sea.

After breakfast we stacked our bags in the hallway ready to be loaded onto the van. The plan was that Megan, Richard and George would walk to the harbour where we would be meeting up with Mark our pilot and his crew. April would be driving Cathy and me in the van with all the kit. The reason I was travelling in the van was because my knee was still very painful and my walking pace so slow. They wanted to make sure I at least got to the start line. Sam would also be meeting us at the harbour along with our two official observers from the British Long Distance Swimming Association.

Our two observers were Kate Robarts and Neil Brinkworth. They were both very experienced open-water swimmers and

I had known them via Facebook for quite some time although I had never actually met either of them. Kate had completed a solo English Channel swim in 2014 and went on to achieve other marathon swims, which earned her the 'Triple Crown of Open Water Swimming'. Neil had also accomplished an English Channel solo swim in 2019, along with many other open-water swims. Both Kate and Neil had also been members of relay swims across the English Channel. We clearly had two great swimmers with a wealth of open-water experience to observe and ratify our attempt.

Our observers Kate Robarts and Neil Brinkworth.

As we travelled along the promenade in the van, we saw Megan, Richard and George walking along the path. April beeped the horn and we laughed and waved as we passed by. We drove into the car park and could see our escort boat *Celtic Fox* which was moored along the far wall of the harbour. April drove the van up a narrow strip, which took us as close as possible to our boat. The three of us then began to unload all our baggage and stack it up alongside the steps that would take us down to the boat.

Megan, Richard and George turned up a few minutes later and helped to unload the last few bags. I then had a text from Sam, which said she had just arrived in the car park with Neil. I replied to tell her that we were already at the boat.

We saw Sam and Neil walking towards us and there were many handshakes, hugs and introductions. None of us had met Neil before, but maybe more remarkably, Sam and Megan had never met, and they were just about to board a boat which would take us all to the start line of a world-first swim attempt. As I witnessed Sam and Megan greeting each other, I couldn't help having a little chuckle and promising myself that one day I may be able to organize a relay team that could actually practise together or at least meet up before embarking on such a major swim.

Kate then turned up and there were more greetings and introductions. I looked around at everyone on the quayside. There were smiles all around and it filled me with joy that the whole team, as well as our observers,

Can I have a hand with my luggage please?

were actually all in the same place at the same time and this swim was finally going to happen.

We then became aware of a lorry that was slowly making its way towards us along this very narrow road. We moved our bags as close as we could towards the edge of the harbour wall to give the lorry a few more inches to negotiate its passage. The lorry stopped just beyond *Celtic Fox* and then it all became clear why it was making this journey. This was the tanker that was about to fill our escort boat up with the fuel it needed to take us to the Isles of Scilly and back. At that sight, it really felt like it was all coming together, and it also felt very real and rather daunting.

Next, we met our pilot Mark and his crew Fred Buckingham and Andy Bennetts. These were the people that were hopefully going to navigate our team of swimmers from Cornwall to the Isles of Scilly. Our team may have all trained our hearts out in the pool, in lakes and in the sea over the last couple of years, but if these three men did not do their job well, then we would not make it across this stretch of ocean. What's more, these were three men we had never met before. We also knew they had very limited experience in piloting swimmers along the route we were taking. However, we had willingly handed a lot of money over to this crew in the hope that they could pull it off for us. This was all to do with trust. To be honest, the crew didn't really need to trust in our ability to be able to swim to the Isles of Scilly. They would get their money if we were successful or not. But we needed to trust in them, that they could give us the best chance of success. Within minutes of meeting them, I had that gut feeling that our crew were honest men who genuinely wanted to be a part of our swimming adventure. Our team of six had increased to a team of eight on meeting our observers and had now swelled to a team of eleven as we welcomed our crew. I was also thrilled when Fred told me he would be writing his own report of our swim, in addition to our official observers' report.

Eleven people, most of whom were meeting each other for the very first time, were about to spend a whole day together on a small boat. We would have to get to know one another, support each other and hopefully form some bonds, but most importantly we all needed to trust each other. The whole challenge depended on this if it had any chance of success. We would share a kettle; we would

Our amazing boat crew. From left: Andy Bennetts,
Mark Johns and Fred Buckingham.

share clothes, and we would also share a toilet that was smaller than the average wardrobe. This was a very intimate affair with total strangers, but if we could just get it right, then maybe everything would fall into place, and we would achieve our goal.

I have swum solo across the English Channel, and it was tough. However, a relay swim is very tough in many different ways. A solo swim requires a huge amount of endurance with regards to the distance you must swim and also dealing with the cold water temperatures for such a prolonged period of time. There is also the issue of feeding while in the water which is not necessary during a relay swim. However, with a relay you have a lot of time on the boat in-between swims, and this can be very challenging in itself. Firstly, on exiting the water, you have a period of trying to warm up again and getting into some dry clothes. It is a lovely feeling once this is achieved, but by then, you have already eaten well into the first hour and you now only have about four hours before you have to reverse the process and get back into your swim gear and into that cold sea for another hour. You don't properly have the chance to relax as you always have your next swim on your mind. This is also when the sea sickness is likely to kick in. At a time when you need to replace your expended energy with some food, you may not feel like eating at all; or if you manage to consume some sustenance, it may not stay in your stomach for long before the fish get their share of it. In no time at all you are starting to get ready for your second swim. Once your second swim is over, the very idea of getting in yet again for a third time is almost unfathomable. Please don't think that relays are easy because you would be a fool to do so.

At around 08:30 we started to load all our bags onto the boat. The steps leading down to *Celtic Fox* were very steep and narrow and so we formed a human chain from the quayside, down the steps and onto the boat and passed the bags between us. Before long *Celtic Fox* was loaded with what looked like enough luggage for a cruise around the world. We all knew we had to take the bare minimum and I think we all achieved that, but once it was all put together on a small boat, it just looked like we had far too much for a day trip out on the sea.

Once we were all on board, our pilot Mark gave us a general talk on housekeeping. Mark was the owner of *Celtic Fox* and so he was ultimately in charge while we were guests on his boat. We were hoping to head off to the start of our swim at that point, but there was a slight delay as there was not enough gas on the boat and we had to wait for another gas cylinder to be delivered. It wasn't long before it arrived and it was greeted by a cheer from all on board. Mark said, "You're no longer rationed on tea and coffee!"

At 09:10 we finally started to head out of Penzance harbour and make our way to our starting point at Nanjizal beach. I looked at the rest of the team who were scattered around the boat and looking out to sea, and at that point, except for Sam, they all appeared to be deep in thought and quite serious. There was an eerie silence on board apart from the sound of the waves crashing against the side of *Celtic Fox* and Sam talking on her phone. Maybe the reality of the situation had finally struck us all simultaneously and we were contemplating our fate.

Neil captures the moment perfectly.

The reason Sam was on the phone was because she was being interviewed live on BBC Radio Cornwall. After a short while everyone appeared to start relaxing a bit and enjoy the wonderful view as we glided past the southern Cornish coastline. Landmarks were pointed out and photos were taken. Sam stood at the back of the boat and her smiles and laughs showed me that her interview was going well. Then as the interview came to an end, Sam announced that the DJ had asked for a cheer from the team, and we all obliged.

As we skimmed across the fresh blue water, just a little further along the coastline a very familiar view came into sight. It was the

All posing for the camera while Sam is interviewed by Radio Cornwall.

Minack theatre sitting high on the clifftop and beneath it was the wonderful golden sands of Porthcurno beach.

Several years previously, I had enjoyed a wonderful day on that beach with Cherie and the kids. We had ventured up the narrow, steep path that took us to a point where we had a good view of the theatre. Then it was back down to the beach for some fun in the sea. Scott, Sean, and I went exploring on our bodyboards while Phoebe stayed on the beach where she had made a new friend. We wanted to see what was around the outcrop of rock to our left. We had already seen the other side from the top of the cliff, but this side remained a bit of a mystery. We paddled out far enough to be clear of the rocks and then began heading across and around this small piece of headland. We were sure it was just going to be more rocks and then we would have to head back slightly disappointed. However, as the new view came into sight it was more wonderful than I could have imagined. There in front of us was a small secluded sandy beach which was completely deserted. What made it all the more stunning was the waterfall at the back of the cove, which cascaded down from somewhere out of the cliff face and onto the beach. It was like something out of a fairytale. We excitedly landed and began to explore. A while later we made the decision that instead of returning via the sea, we would instead climb over the rocks whilst carrying our bodyboards to get back to Porthcurno beach. This was another adventure in itself, but eventually, we returned to Cherie, who was guarding the towels and bags, and she seemed very relieved that we had all made it back in one piece.

Megan putting on a brave face on the way to the start.

As *Celtic Fox* continued its journey to the start, I could feel the nervous excitement build amongst the team. We all clearly had a barrage of thoughts and emotions whirling around inside us, so it was important to focus on the positive and try hard to suppress the negative. The pressure of being a part of a six-person team cannot be underestimated. None of us wanted to be the weakest link. To be the person that let the whole team down and be the reason we were unsuccessful. These thoughts needed to be taken to a safe place in our minds and locked away so they could not escape and cause havoc and ultimately jeopardize the whole swim.

Eventually, the boat turned north-west around Gwennap Head and very soon Land's End came into view in the distance. Our starting point on the cliff face near Nanjizal beach was now visible and we were speeding towards it. Now that we could actually see for the first time where our swim would begin, and looking out over the vast ocean ahead, the enormity of what we were about to take on really hit us. Six Scilly Swimmers were about to embark on a relay swim that had never been done before. We were literally heading into the unknown.

I was still trying to enjoy the stunning view of this stretch of the Cornish coastline, but now I had to focus on the task at hand. Under a cloudless sky, the water looked so calm and inviting, but we knew that it may not stay that way. We saw some other boats out there going about their business. I bet none of them were engaged in anything quite as exciting as us! The start line was rapidly approaching, and Sam was already getting changed into her swim costume, ready to begin our adventure.

Celtic Fox started to head inland, and I suddenly realized that the view in front of me was indeed Nanjizal beach. This was where Megan's partner Mark and their son Owen, as well as Cathy's parents Liz and Ian, were planning to see us off. We were heading to the cliff face just left of Nanjizal Beach. I had studied our starting point on

Google Maps many times and always assumed it would be a beach start, and this is what I had prepared for. However, the rock face we were heading for was clearly a better starting point, distance wise. Unfortunately, it meant those that had come to see us off would now have to do so from a distance and I did wonder if any of them had brought a pair of binoculars.

Our start point on the cliff face just left of Nanjizal beach.

Sam stood on the deck in her swim costume, hat and goggles, looking a little nervous although still smiling. You could feel the excitement and anticipation in the air that everyone on board was experiencing. Mark took *Celtic Fox* as close as possible to the start point and then explained the topography to Sam and pointed out a very small area at the foot of the cliff where there were no breaking waves. This was where it was the safest place to start the swim. Sam would have to touch the rock face to officially begin our relay. It wasn't that easy to see this from the boat, but once in the water it would be even more difficult for Sam to navigate her way to this precise position at sea level. Kate then explained the strict rules regarding our changeovers, just to make sure everyone was perfectly clear on them.

Sam is ready for the challenge and about to swim to the start.

Sam made some final adjustments to her goggles as she prepared to enter the water and head to the start, and we all wished her good luck. Then, to everyone's amusement, she turned to me and said, "I'm only doing this if there's going to be a book about it!"

I laughed and replied, "Of course."

As Sam dived into the sea and began making her way to our starting point, I realized I had now made a proper commitment to writing a book about this swimming adventure of ours. Now all we needed to do was to succeed so that my book would have the perfect ending.

ELEVEN

THE ADVENTURE BEGINS

Round One:

We all watched with excitement as Sam glided through the deep blue water and made her way to the start of our swim. As she approached the cliff face, she appeared to slow down and was clearly trying to negotiate a safe passage to the wall of rock in front of her. Sam needed to touch the rock in order to officially begin the swim at mainland Britain.

Moments later we could see that Sam had stopped and then her arm waved in the air to signify she had made contact with the mainland. Mark sounded the boat's horn to officially start the swim and the time was recorded at 10:06:10.

Sam began making her way back towards *Celtic Fox* and was looking strong in the water with a stroke rate of 59/min. The air temperature was 21°C (68.9°F); sea temperature was 17°C (62.6°F), and the wind speed was 6kts from the north-west. The conditions were certainly looking very favorable at this point.

Everyone cheered as Sam passed the boat to starboard. This was our pilot Mark's preferred side for us to swim on so that it gave him the best view of us in the water. Both swimmer and pilot will have their preferences as to which side of the boat they want the swim to take place, but ultimately the pilot has the final say. Us swimmers may have a favourite side of the boat for our swim, but it is the pilot's responsibility to keep the swimmer safe, and that takes precedence over everything.

Observer's report 10:06: 'Mark and Andy hoist the day shapes and flag Alpha. Fred explains the shapes and colours to the swimmers.'

As Sam headed out of our familiar English Channel and into the Atlantic Ocean, I contemplated the fact that none of the team had ever swum in the Atlantic Ocean before. I realized that not only was this going to be a world-first relay attempt, but it was also a first for all of us swimming in this expanse of water. It was a really big deal for everyone, and this relay swim was such a major task for us to even attempt, let alone accomplish.

Observer's report 10:23: 'A yacht passes in front of the bow, heading towards Longships. Sam maintains a 5m distance from the boat. S/R (stroke rate per minute) 65.'

One thing I don't think any of us were expecting was just how large the swell could get out there. A little way into Sam's swim we became aware the swell was picking up, but in no time at all we were looking ahead to huge walls of water slowly approaching us. These liquid mountains were very intimidating but at the same time a totally awesome experience; it was like navigating our way over the Himalayan foothills. The sight of how the ocean had decided to present itself to us on this particular day was actually quite scary if I'm honest but at the same time very exhilarating!

It's funny because many times in the past, if I had been a bit slow with a particular swim, I would joke that it was mostly uphill. Obviously, I had no real concept that swimming uphill could really occur; it was just said in fun. However, right then I was actually witnessing Sam swimming uphill against gravity. She would then reach the peak and begin the descent on the other side before the next mountain reached her. It was a totally breathtaking sight and I had never witnessed anything like it before. Sam and I had previously run a couple of marathons together and I know she was no fan of running up hills. But swimming uphill was taking things to a completely different level and I knew Sam was not going to be impressed!

Towards the end of Sam's swim the sea decided to flatten out a bit and behave itself, much to the relief of all of us. It was then that we heard an ominous sound in the distance, and as it got louder we noticed a helicopter approaching from the mainland. It was the local coastguards on a training exercise who were coming to show us their support. They obviously knew about our relay swim

Megan capturing the moment.

because Cathy was a winch paramedic for the coast guard in Kent. The helicopter circled us several times with the doors open and the crew waving at us. Sam briefly turned onto her back so she could witness the spectacle and then continued with her swim. The helicopter then returned one last time and hovered very low above us. As it started to fly back to the mainland, Sam raised her head out of the water and shouted, "Fucking epic!"

This comment from Sam greatly amused us and there was lots of laughter on board the boat. Luckily, I had managed to film this moment and Sam's comment while swimming. It's a very treasured memory.

Sam waving at the coastguard crew in appreciation of their support.

Richard was now standing at the back of the boat in his trunks and ready to take over from Sam. As he stood there fiddling with his goggles, he looked confident and well up for this challenge. Sam had made great progress during her swim and we all knew Richard would do the same.

The whistle was blown and Sam's hour was over. Richard jumped into the water and started to swim out behind Sam as she made her way back to the boat. Sam climbed up the ladder to join us, with a huge grin on her face. She was more than happy with how her swim had gone but also elated about the coastguard's fly-past. Sam had previously been a volunteer for the coastguard in Kent as well as the Royal National Lifeboat Institution (RNLI).

Richard went storming off like he always does. There was still a huge swell but luckily not much chop so Richard wouldn't really notice at sea level the massive watery 'hills' he was swimming over.

Observer's report 11:06: 'First changeover. Richard in, Sam out. She is a happy swimmer and elated about the fly-past. Richard S/R66. Sam says "That's the longest I've swum without stopping or moaning!" Richard settles into a great pace and maintains his distance of about 5m from the boat.'

I stood on the deck, leaning on the warm metal railing and watching Richard swim. There is something very special about viewing someone swimming in the sea. I had seen Richard swimming in a pool probably thousands of times over the years since we were kids. But put him in the sea and it takes on a whole new meaning. If I'm honest, Richard doesn't have the most graceful style of swimming, but he does have power and determination, and that's all we can really ask from any of our team. I really enjoyed watching Richard powering through the water and looking so strong.

With the warm sun beaming down on me and the boat gently rocking back and forth, it was easy to relax and forget why I was there. Every so often I would check the time as I knew I was next in the water at 12:06 promptly. With about twenty minutes to go I decided it was time to stop being a spectator and start to prepare myself for being a participant.

> Observer's report 11:48: 'A trawler passes the bow. Mark is getting ready for his first leg. A bit of breeze is evident now and there is some surface movement.'

I got changed into my trunks and swim hat and took some last-minute carbs and fluid. It was almost time for me to take over from Richard, and as always, I felt very nervous. Apart from Sam, I was the most experienced open-water swimmer on the team, but this doesn't stop the nerves kicking in. I was experiencing so many intrusive negative thoughts about being the one to completely mess things up for the whole team and let everyone down, and that I would be a huge disappointment to everyone. This is the reason doing a relay can be more stressful than a solo, because at least with a solo you only have yourself to let down and nobody else.

With a couple of minutes to go, I stood there adjusting my goggles when I noticed Kate looking at me. It was a look of concern. Then she said to me, "Mark, you're going to have to remove that tape on your knee."

To be honest I had completely forgotten it was there. Phoebe had taped my knee up two days previously to help me walk and it had definitely helped with the pain. But now Kate explained that it could be seen as an aid to my swimming and so it should be removed. I had no problem with this and could completely understand where she was coming from. As I peeled the tape off, I had to laugh as I had obviously caught the sun a bit and there was now an image of the tape where my skin was much paler.

Richard completes his first swim.

Andy came to the back of the boat, ready to assist me with my changeover with Richard. I stood there, still messing about with my goggles as swimmers do. The boat slowed and a whistle was blown for Richard to stop and for me to take over. Andy opened the bar at the back of the boat and I stepped down onto the small platform, ready to begin my swim. I looked out at the gorgeous blue Atlantic Ocean and the view was both inviting and terrifying at the same time. I knew this was my time to shine. I had to just get in there and swim my heart out for the next hour.

Fred's report: 'We learnt that Mark had completed the Brighton Marathon just three days before. What would this do to his energy reserves?'

Richard heard the whistle and put his head up to look at the boat for confirmation that his hour stint was over. At this point I jumped off the platform and into the sea. The feeling was totally exhilarating as I was plunged into the cold salty water of the Atlantic Ocean. As I surfaced and took a huge breath of air, I thought to myself, *this is it. It's time to crack on and do my part for the team.*

I always thought to myself that my entrance into the sea was never as glamourous as my teammates'. I did find it curious that all the female members of the team decided to dive into the water, while the males all jumped in. Richard and George both had a specific way of jumping in due to their lifeguard background. I simply jumped and plummeted deep into the water before resurfacing and then I was away.

Observer's report 12:06: 'Mark in, Richard out. Richard is happy with his swim.'

My first priority was to calm my breathing right down and get my stroke into a good rhythm. I managed to establish this fairly quickly and was pleased I had got stuck into this swim without any dramas. The sea conditions at this point were good and I glided through the water with relative ease.

As I relaxed into the swim, my mind had more free time to do as it pleased. This isn't always a good thing when swimming in a deep ocean. I remembered my recent conversation with Cathy when she told me she had just been on the phone to our pilot Mark and he was out on the boat, shark spotting with tourists. The inevitable intrusive thoughts of what may be lurking about in the depths below me started to kick in. I have always struggled to keep these kinds of thoughts under control while swimming in the English Channel, but now I was in the Atlantic Ocean, so they seemed to be more frightening. Just saying the words 'Atlantic Ocean' immediately feels more intimidating and threatening than the English Channel. This ocean was mind-blowingly vast, and I couldn't even begin to fathom how deep it was. What this meant was that there were undoubtedly more sea inhabitants out there than I could ever imagine. Huge creatures must certainly be moving about quietly below me. Would they decide to come and investigate what was splashing about on the surface? Would they be friendly? Would they have massive gaping mouths encrusted with thousands of razor-sharp teeth? "STOP IT NOW!" I shouted to myself in my head.

As someone who suffers with anxiety, it was so important to keep my thoughts under control. How would I ever be able to live with myself if the relay failed because I had a panic attack and couldn't breathe because I thought I may be eaten by a shark? I simply had to remain calm and divert my thoughts elsewhere.

Then suddenly, Joan popped into my head, which was a very pleasant surprise. Joan was a resident I had been caring for over the previous couple of years. She was our eldest resident at the home I worked in and fast approaching her hundredth birthday. Joan was a kind and lovely person but also a very straight talker and would soon put anyone in their place if she thought it was necessary. We had a great connection and she loved talking to me about all sorts of things while I helped her with her daily shower. Strangely, the one thing that never came up in conversation was swimming. That was until one day, when I took her to the hairdresser, and while we waited, she mentioned that she used to love swimming. I was thrilled she had announced this and told her I was a swimmer too. Joan then informed me that she used to belong to the Bury St Edmunds Swimming Club; the very same club that I was a proud member of for many years. Obviously, Joan was a member well before my time, but I loved the thought that we were both in the same swimming club. Joan told me she hadn't stopped swimming until she was ninety-one years old. She looked so happy and proud of me when I told her that I had somehow managed to swim across the English Channel.

Joan and I would often talk about what she would want to do on her hundredth birthday. Clearly, she wanted to celebrate with family and friends, but she also made me promise something. Although Joan could not stand without assistance anymore, she made me promise that I would have a dance with her on her birthday to celebrate reaching the grand age of a hundred. I was not quite sure how practical this would be, but I obviously had to agree to the promise.

As her birthday approached, Joan became very unwell, and it wasn't long before she was on end-of-life care. Just days before her hundredth birthday I went in to see her after I had finished my shift. She looked so ill and was on a lot of medication to keep her comfortable. I held her hand and she gave me a smile. She was too weak to talk but she gave me a look that showed me that she recognized me. I reminded her that it was only a few days until our planned dance together and she just continued to look at me and smile. I finally had to bid her goodnight and left.

I arrived at work early the following morning with only one person on my mind. I was informed straight away that Joan had passed away peacefully during the night. I was glad that she was no longer unwell, but at the same time I was gutted that she never made it to her special birthday or had a dance with me.

Joan passed away just a couple of weeks before our relay and now, while I was swimming through the water, I was thinking about her. I was convinced that Joan was watching me and cheering me on as a fellow swimmer. By popping into my mind, she had also helped me to divert my thoughts away from the negative and scary images that I was experiencing and onto something more positive and focused. I felt happy that Joan was able to help me during my swim because I knew that's exactly what she would have wanted to do. Right then, I felt nothing but love and admiration for this amazing lady.

> Observer's report: 'Mark S/R65, swimming a little further away at around 10m and maintaining it. Long swell evident again.'

I now felt much more relaxed and could actually start to enjoy my swim. The beams of sunlight piercing the water looked totally magnificent as my hands glided through them in front of me. There were so many jellyfish moving majestically below and lots of varieties I had never seen before. Although I was well aware of the dangers of certain jellyfish to humans and also had first-hand experience of the pain they could inflict on us, I still welcomed the sight of them and loved watching their graceful movement. It was simply mesmerizing.

> Observer's report: 'Mark moves closer to the boat. He's making headway at 1.5kts into 0.8kts of tide.'

As usual I lost complete track of time while I was absorbed in my own little aquatic world. Eventually, I noticed George on the deck in his swim hat and realized that I was getting towards the end of my first swim. Then I saw frantic waving from the boat and that signified I had just ten minutes of my swim left. This was also a sign for me to up my game and push that little bit harder to ensure I used every bit of energy I possessed to make the best possible progress for the team.

I powered through the water using all my strength and energy, knowing that it would only be a few minutes before I was back on the boat and resting. Then suddenly I heard the whistle being blown and I looked up to get confirmation from my team that my swim had ended and it was now time to head directly back to the boat and allow George to swim around the back of me and continue our relay.

I swum over to the back of our escort boat and as it rocked quite violently in the water, I grabbed hold of the railings on each side of the steps and hauled myself out of the sea. Kate gave me a helping hand to get back on board, and although I mostly enjoyed my swim, I was still glad that it was over for another five hours. Then the inevitable happened and I began to shiver. Over the years I had actually got to quite enjoy the shivering process. I knew my body was hypothermic as it had been countless times before. I also knew that shivering was my body's natural coping mechanism and

Glad to have completed my first swim.

was going to increase my core temperature back to near a normal range. I was happy to sit there shivering for however long it took. My team were also happy with this as they knew this was normal for me. The crew, however, needed some convincing that I was fine and did not require any medical intervention.

> Observer's report 13:06: 'George in, Mark out. Changeovers are efficient and well executed. Mark is extremely shivery and the team, well used to this reaction from him, set about to warm him up, getting him into as many layers as possible and giving him a hot drink. They reassure Mark, Andy and Fred that Mr Ransom always reacts like this and that it's nothing to worry about.'

I had only got to see George swimming very briefly at the start of his stint as I was very soon consumed with my warming-up process. What I did see was that George was out there, looking strong and determined in the water like he always does. That was all I needed to see, and it gave me enough reassurance that the job was getting done.

> Observer's report: 'Another trawler passes the boat to stern. George S/R67 and settling into his swim.'

Eventually, I was dry and dressed and emerged back onto the deck, still shaking a little. I was delighted to see George still powering through the water. He was now well into his hour and Megan was already preparing for her first swim.

The sun was still beating down on us, which is very welcome when you're in the sea, as long as you have put your sunscreen on. Luckily, we were all prepared for the hot sun. The sea was not as calm as it had previously been but still not posing any real problems for us.

Megan stood on the deck in her costume, hat and goggles. She looked quite nervous and rightly so. The rest of us all had previous experience of swimming out in the sea next to an escort boat, but this was a complete first for Megan. Also, apart from seeing Megan have a little casual swim the previous day, I had never actually seen her swim properly. I was both excited and nervous to see Megan out there because I really didn't know what to expect. She was the 'unknown' to me and most of the team.

Fred's report: 'We could all feel the infectious excitement of Megan as she prepared for her first hour.'

Megan looking totally focused and ready for this challenge.

Suddenly the whistle was blown to inform George that his hour had finished and I saw Megan standing on the small platform ready to begin. George started heading back towards the boat, and without any hesitation, Megan dived into the water. She briefly raised her head to get her bearings and then raced off, passing behind George and off across the ocean.

Observer's report 14:06: 'Megan in, George out. George enjoyed his swim. Megan goes off like a rocket. S/R74. This is her first-time swimming beside an escort boat. Her stroke settles down to 70 as she finds her position and maintains it. The tanker Opaline comes across the bow at 16kts. There is quite a lot of cloud cover now and the sun had disappeared. Megan is swimming strongly.'

George finishes his first hour.

As I watched Megan powering through the water, and studied her swimming technique, I felt really confident in her ability. The way she moved her arms, the way she kicked her legs and also her method of breathing. Although Megan was not an experienced open-water swimmer, I was so impressed at how well she was doing. It was also very evident that Megan had that very determined streak in her to succeed.

Fred's report: 'Watching these athletes in the water was a joy. Their adaptations to deal with the conditions were seamless. The economy of motion, the body showing the skills acquired after years of training and the brain set and determination. On autopilot but adapting to the waves and the heading of the boat, the determination to do their best, the pleasure of swimming and working as a team. Poetry in motion, with the speed and grace of an animal that lives in the water.'

By now, the nausea really started to kick in and I wasn't the only one experiencing this. Being on a small boat out in the sea is one thing, but when it is travelling at such a slow speed, it really is at the mercy of the waves. The up and down motion as well as the rocking from side to side is relentless. We had plenty of food, but we struggled to decide what we could actually stomach.

Cathy preparing for her first swim.

As Cathy started to get ready for her swim, Megan was still maintaining a great pace. In no time at all, Cathy stood on the back platform, and as the whistle was blown for Megan to stop, Cathy dived straight in and swam around the back of Megan as she headed back to the boat. Megan climbed back on board with a look on her face like she had just had the swim of her life.

> Observer's report 15:06: 'Cathy in, Megan out. A brilliant first relay swim by Megan. Cathy S/R52. She's looking relaxed and graceful and gliding through the water. The sky is a little brighter.'

There is something very relaxing about watching Cathy swim. Her slow, delicate stroke does not reflect that dogged determination to get the job done, which we all knew was inbuilt in her. While watching Cathy smoothly coasting through the water, you would never believe she also played rugby. Put her on a field with a rugby ball and she would show her aggressive side, but place her in the water and she had the grace and elegance of a ballet dancer. It was simply a beautiful sight to witness.

Cathy gliding through the water.

Cathy did not falter at all during her swim and just kept pushing forwards and getting us closer to our target end point. Just after the ten-minute signal was given to Cathy for her to finish, we all heard a very familiar sound. A low vibrating noise that was gradually getting louder. As we looked out over the ocean, we saw that the coastguard helicopter was making a return visit to show their support. This was such an uplifting moment, and we were so pleased that Cathy was swimming at the time they returned.

The helicopter flew right above us and then circled a couple of times. The side door was open and the coastguard crew were waving at us as we waved back. Cathy paused briefly in the water to also wave at them. It was a real morale booster to get this support from the coastguard helicopter crew.

One last fly-past to wish us good luck.

Observer's report 16:02: 'The CG helicopter returns just inttime to see Cathy in the water. They circle and she waves. The crew are in the doorway, waving to her.'

Although being distracted by the helicopter fly-past, we were also aware that Sam was now in her costume and ready to start the next round of our relay. We were now almost six hours into this swim and so far, all was going very well for us.

Round Two:

I could hardly believe we had all swum already, it had gone so quickly, and that Sam was getting ready to get back in the sea and do it all over again. We were now well into the afternoon; the sun was not as present as it had been and the sea appeared to be getting a little irritated with us. I think Neptune had finally twigged what we were up to and had decided to test us to see how tough we really were.

Sam prepared herself on the platform while the whistle was blown for Cathy to finish and make her way back to the boat. Sam dived in and another perfect transition was executed. Round two of our relay had begun.

Getting back in the sea for the second time is not always easy, especially as you have that nagging thought in the back of your mind that it won't be the last time. Another hour of swimming in cold water, and it would not be as pleasant or exciting as the first. The sea had upped its game and had developed a certain chop that did not make it easy to get into any kind of rhythm or even breathe efficiently. Despite this, Sam just continued swimming like she always does.

Observer's report 16:06: 'Sam is in for second rotation, Cathy out. Cathy is very happy and says that the CG arrived just when she needed a boost. Sam S/R61. There's now quite a headwind from SW and Sam is swimming straight into it, with occasional white caps breaking over her.'

Kate meticulously making notes.

By now, the nausea was really getting to us. I knew I had to eat but I really didn't want to put anything in my mouth. As I stood there on the deck feeling sorry for myself, I suddenly saw Megan launch herself at the side of the boat. Richard and I both instinctively grabbed hold of her because she looked like she was about to go overboard. Megan vomited over the railings while we held on to her. The reality of a very long relay swim was certainly making itself known.

With Megan now safe, having emptied her stomach, I now took to standing on the deck and leaning over with my head resting on my hands. The gentle rocking of the boat was relentless. I felt like I needed to vomit but simply couldn't. I also knew I needed to get some food inside me as a source of energy for my next swim. George came over to see if he could help in some way. He asked me what I wanted to eat. I could only think about one thing right then, and that was a chicken and mushroom Pot Noodle. One of my favourite snacks ever and certainly the one that would hopefully make me feel better. George said he would prepare my Pot Noodle for me, and I was so grateful of this, as I certainly could not stomach going inside where the kettle was. It's a very strange thing with sea sickness; for some reason it gets a lot worse if you go down into the boat or inside in any way.

George returned with my choice of food. I still didn't feel like eating anything, but this was probably the best chance I had of getting some kind of sustenance inside me. After letting it cool a little, I took my fork and wound some noodles around it. This was a snack I absolutely adored, but right then I really wasn't sure how I would react to eating it. I put my first forkful in my mouth. It was bland and chewy. I kept trying to convince myself that this was a delicious treat for me, but my senses were telling me otherwise. As I swallowed, I was already winding more noodles around my fork. Again, I put it in my mouth and started the now difficult task of chomping on it. I chewed away on my mouthful of noodles for way longer than I usually would, because I was deliberately delaying the inevitable swallowing process. I just wasn't convinced my stomach would welcome any more of my favourite treat. I finally plucked up the courage to swallow what was in my mouth, and seconds later I regretted it. All of a sudden, my nausea became worse, and I developed an intense dislike for chicken and mushroom Pot Noodle. In fact, I came to the conclusion that if this was the case, then I had probably developed a dislike for all food in general.

There was no way I could possibly put another forkful of noodles in my mouth, with a serious intention of swallowing it. I walked to the side of the boat and tipped the contents of my plastic pot into the sea. My reasoning was that if I ate the noodles, I would definitely vomit and feed the fish. So, I may as well cut out the middleman and put the noodles directly into the water so the fish could enjoy a tasty snack without the added ingredients of my stomach acid. I then returned to my spot and again rested my head on my hands and felt even more sorry for myself as the boat continued to rock from side to side.

Observer's report 16:50: 'The sea is flattening out just a little, enough to allow Sam to breathe more easily and experience less of a slap in the face. A Fulmar has been circling her. Observer pulls a face at her and Ms Jones gives her famous "salute". Richard is preparing for his second swim.'

Realizing that the ten-minute signal had been given to Sam, I suddenly felt a wave of guilt sweep over me. Because of my nausea and self-pity, I had almost completely missed watching Sam on her second swim, so I forced myself to move to the side of the boat so that I could watch Sam doing what she does best. She looked as awesome as ever in the water, just as I expected she would.

Richard was ready to go in and looked as fresh as when we had started. The whistle was blown, and Richard entered the sea while Sam made her way back to the boat. By now it felt like our swim was well and truly making good progress. However, we also knew that as more time passed, this swim would inevitably become more difficult for us all, and there would also be a greater chance of something happening that could put a stop to the challenge.

Observer's report 17:06: 'Richard in, Sam out. Richard S/ R65. Sam climbs up the ladder and pauses at the top to say, "Are my tits in?", making the team laugh and slightly disconcerting Andy, who's getting ready to close the gate behind her.'

Fred's report: 'When you spend a day on a boat and all the passengers talk about is swimming, you begin to understand their total commitment to their sport. The time spent, the friendships made, the technique, the teamwork, the training, the sacrifices required, the expense, the devotion and the sheer physical and mental courage required.'

As the boat chugged its way across the Atlantic Ocean, the sun was still shining, and morale was strong in the team. Richard was delivering exactly what we expected him to. However, it was now Sam's turn to be cursed with the dreaded sea sickness. All of a sudden, she was vomiting over the back of the boat. I think it must have come on so quickly that Sam didn't really have time to think about which side of the boat she should lean over to empty her stomach. As a result, Sam vomited all over the small platform that we used to start our swims. Unfortunately, the platform was just a little too high out of the water for the sea to wash her sick away. As I was the next swimmer to go in, I faced the prospect that I would begin my swim by standing in Sam's vomit. As I have said many times before, there is no glamour in this sport.

> Observer's report 17:42: 'Dolphin time. Several of them are swimming at the bow and then decide to swim around and under Richard, much to the excitement of those on the boat. Richard looks like he's smiling but nobody knows if he has spotted them.'

I started to get changed into my trunks and mentally prepare myself for another hour in the sea. The inevitable nerves kicked in, but I tried to keep them at bay and stay focused on the task at hand. Richard got his ten-minute signal and I was standing on the deck ready to begin.

> Observer's report 17:56: '10 minute warning and Richard gives the thumbs up. A small light aircraft flies directly overhead.'

We still had plenty of light so I would not require any light sticks attached to me for this hour. However, when George followed on from me, he would need some light sticks as his swim was not due to finish until 20:06 and light could well be fading by then, depending on cloud cover.

This would be my last swim in daylight. I knew my next one would be starting just after midnight, but I really didn't want to think that far ahead. One swim at a time is all we should be focusing on. If I had to do a third daylight swim, then things would have gone very horribly wrong, and we would probably have missed the Isles of Scilly and be heading towards America.

The whistle was blown for Richard to stop swimming and allow me to take over. I felt as ready as I could be, and as the gate was opened for me, I stepped down onto the platform, and also into Sam's vomit. I couldn't help thinking that it was a good job Sam and I were close friends and had shared so much over the years. Maybe this was taking it a little too far though!

I once again jumped into the cold sea and felt myself submerge a few feet before I rose to the surface and took a gasp of breath. I spotted Richard a short distance away and swum towards him. As we passed in the water, I couldn't help thinking to myself that poor Richard was completely oblivious to the fact that he was just about to endure the platform of vomit as he made his way back onto the boat. I also found this very amusing.

Observer's report 18:06: 'Mark in, Richard out. He's been stung a few times by compass jellies but says he neither heard nor saw the dolphins playing alongside him.'

I was just starting to get into a rhythm when something unusual happened. The left side of my goggles started to fill with water. At first it was just annoying, but it continued to fill until I was forced to stop and empty it. Obviously, as soon as I stopped, there was concern from the team on the boat and I was asked if I was alright. I reassured them that I was fine but just had some water in my goggles. I continued swimming.

Within a few more minutes, my goggles started to fill up again. I didn't know what was going on as this very rarely happened to me while simply swimming. I remembered there had been the odd occasion while training for my solo down in Dover that I had collided with an oncoming swimmer and had to readjust my goggles, but this was very unusual. Not wanting to lose any time I decided to close my left eye and continue swimming. However, I found this very weird and not comfortable at all. Having spent several decades swimming with both eyes open, just that small change to my routine by having one eye closed had completely thrown me. I simply couldn't carry on like this and had to pause once again.

I made sure that this stop to empty my goggles was as brief as possible. Firstly, I didn't want to lose any time and secondly, I didn't want there to be enough time for anyone to question why I had stopped again. Then I quickly got my head down and continued with my swim.

Imagine my disbelief and frustration when my goggles were filling with water for the third time and forcing me to stop. By now the team were quite concerned about me having to stop yet again and asked what the problem was. I told them about my goggle issue and straight away they offered to throw me another pair. I declined this offer as I knew there was nothing wrong with the goggles as they had served me so well up until this moment. I concluded that it must be human error. As I trod water, I decided I needed to sort this problem out once and for all. I felt that I needed to remove my goggles and put them back on again. But just before doing this, I moved my hands around them to see if I could find any obvious problem. As my hands moved along the strap, I realized that it was far too high up on my head and was definitely the reason for my goggles filling up. The strap must have ridden up as I jumped into the sea. This was something that had never happened to me before but clearly it had now. Open-water swimming has a habit of bringing unwanted surprises and sometimes they are very poorly timed!

I repositioned my goggles as they should be and continued swimming. Although I knew I had wasted a small amount of time sorting my goggles out, I also knew that I was happy they were not going to leak anymore and slow me down. I was now satisfied that I could just crack on and swim the best I could until my hour was up.

I found it very comforting to see my jellyfish friends were still on this journey with me. Admittedly, a couple did make contact with my skin and caused a sting, but I was sure that it was not intentional on their part and I certainly didn't hold it against them. After all, I was the one who was trespassing in their domain, so how could I possibly complain. Besides, I always think that a little kiss from a jellyfish is actually quite sweet.

Something that I did notice about this hour compared to my first was that the water felt so much colder. I didn't really know why this would be the case. Obviously, we were further out into the ocean, but I didn't think it would make that much difference. I considered whether it may be down to the fact that I had stopped swimming three times to adjust my goggles. Pausing in the sea will cause your body temperature to start dropping, but I was certain I had not been stationary long enough for it to really affect me. It wasn't until later on that I was told that most of the team felt their second swim was colder than their first.

Receiving my ten-minute warning was very welcome and felt like it was well overdue. By now I was actually beginning to shiver while still in the water. This is never a good thing and was also something that was extremely rare for me. I increased my pace as much as I could to ensure we were that little bit closer to the Isles of Scilly at the end of my hour in the water and also in an attempt to try to raise my body temperature a little.

Then I heard the whistle being blown and saw George jumping into the sea. Finally, my hour was over and I could try to get warm again. I reached the back of the boat and grabbed hold of the rails on each side of the steps. As I hauled myself out of the water, I suddenly realized just how much I was shivering. It really wasn't like me to shiver in the water or immediately on exiting. It usually started just after the euphoria of emerging from the cold water and back into air had subsided.

I stepped back onto the small platform and then remembered about Sam's vomit. It both amused me and disturbed me at the same time. Once I was back on the deck, somebody wrapped my towel around me.

Observer's report 18:56: 'Megan gives Mark the ten-minute warning and Mark acknowledges. In the final ten minutes of his swim, the head on swell just begins to build. He appears to have no further problems with his goggles. During these final ten minutes, the team discuss lights and a green guardian light is attached to George's goggles for his next swim, together with a glow stick on his trunks. It will be light when he gets in but the light is beginning to fade. Another guardian light from Sam's stash will be kept for the next takeover.'

Observer's report 19:06: 'George in, Mark out. As Mark ascends the ladder, he is already shivering and his knees are sore, hardly surprising when he ran the Brighton Marathon on the Sunday before the swim.'

Suddenly, and without any warning, the boat took off at great speed. I was confused and had no idea what was going on. Had the swim been aborted, and we were now heading back to the mainland? No, there was no way that could be the case as I had just witnessed George jump in the water, and I had definitely swum past him. Then a feeling of panic swept over me. Why were we leaving George in the middle of the Atlantic Ocean? What on earth was going on? For a very brief moment I thought that maybe the cold had made me hallucinate and that this wasn't actually happening. Then I heard a voice say, "Make sure you keep eyes on him at all times."

The boat was clearly going around in a huge circle, and I then spotted George out in the sea with his green flashing lights. We were approaching him at some speed and then the boat began to slow as we came closer. Thank God he was safe, and we were once again alongside him.

George later told me that he did not know what was happening either. Apparently, just before getting in, he was instructed to keep swimming towards the sun at all times. I can only imagine what George was feeling as the boat sped away from him and it can't have been good!

It was later explained that the boat had lost position slightly and that doing a circle and coming back alongside George, was the easiest way to get the swim back on course.

Observer's report: 'George adjusts his goggles. He's swimming quite a distance from the boat, making it difficult to see him in the fading light. George adjusts his own position, bringing himself closer, much to the relief of the observers. There are now white horses on the surface but George isn't bothered by them and continues to swim strongly. His S/R is 63. Occasionally, he must swim up and down the face of a wave as the wind starts to build.'

I made my way inside the cabin and sat down with my towel wrapped around me. I was now shivering a huge amount and a dry robe was also placed around me by someone. People were telling me to get dry and changed but I didn't want to move. I remember both Cathy and Sam trying to persuade me to change but I was just so stubborn and was having none of it.

As I sat there shivering and feeling sorry for myself, I became aware of Sam standing right in front of me, and as I glanced up at her, I felt a feeling of concern because she definitely had her 'serious face' on. Sam and I had been friends for many years, and we had shared a lot together, and so I knew exactly what a 'Sam serious face' meant when she was directing it straight at me. This indicated one of two things. She was either pissed off with me or concerned about me for some reason. I couldn't really think why she would be pissed off with me as I didn't think my swim had gone that bad, and even if it had, Sam would not be pissed off, just relieved that I was alright. I then realized it was obviously concern that Sam had. But why would she be concerned? I was sure that she must have seen me in a worse state than this before. She had seen me hypothermic and shivering more times than I could even remember. Sam also knew how well I recovered from a state of hypothermia after a certain amount of time. She was also well aware that I actually enjoyed the feeling of recovering from

Sam and Cathy assisting me to warm up.

hypothermia and the whole process of shivering uncontrollably. I am sure most people would find this a very weird thing to actually experience as something enjoyable, but we all find pleasure in very different ways, and for me, the warming-up process from hypothermia is simply exquisite.

> Observer's report: 'Mark is very cold and being warmed up in the wheelhouse. Richard provides some jazzy fairisle socks for him to wear with his sandals. The look may take off! He says that the goggle problem was caused by the head straps becoming dislodged as he jumped in, and that it took him quite a while to work out what had happened.'

Sam began asking me some questions to ascertain if I was disoriented and confused. The first question she asked was where we were swimming to. I glanced at the hoodie she was wearing, emblazoned with our 'Six Scilly Swimmers' logo. My reply was simple, "The Scilly Isles. It's written on your top."

After some laughter she continued with her questioning and I think I just about passed the test. I may have passed the disorientation test, but I was still very hypothermic and needed to warm up. Much to the annoyance of the rest of the team, I was still being a stubborn bugger and refusing to remove my swim trunks, get dry properly and change into dry clothes.

My logical mind was telling me I should listen to my friends because I knew their advice was spot on and exactly what I would be telling someone else in the same situation. However, right then I just wanted to curl up and shiver and pretend that's all that mattered in life at that moment.

I was given a hot drink to try to warm me up from the inside. I was happy with that and was prepared to drink it as long as everyone just left me alone to shiver. But they didn't leave me alone and Cathy and Sam kept hounding me to get changed into some warm clothes. I knew that what they were demanding of me was the right thing to do but I just didn't want to do it right then.

Eventually they won, and I slipped my wet trunks off and started to get into some dry clothes which were being passed to me. I felt like I was doing it more for them than myself, which was a ridiculous thought really. People can be very ungrateful when their mind isn't thinking straight due to hypothermia. At last, I sat there wearing many dry and warm layers, but the shaking had not yet ceased. I then started to think a bit more about what had just

The team trying to conserve their body heat.

happened and felt a certain amount of guilt at the way I had been so awkward towards my friends, who were simply trying to help me.

> Observer's report: 'As darkness falls, the whole team starts to don more layers, to keep them as warm as possible before facing their night swims.'

I glanced over to the crew who were a few feet to my left. I saw all the sophisticated equipment they had in front of them. One was a screen, which clearly showed our position in the ocean. They knew how far we had come and how much further we had to go. At that moment, the very thought of getting back in that cold ocean just after midnight, for my third swim, was simply unimaginable. How could I possibly endure that cold again and this time in the dark?

I don't think my mind was working logically at this point as I should have known for certain that a third swim was inevitable for me. In a desperate attempt to bring myself some comfort, I asked the crew how far we had to go. The response was not what I wanted or hoped for, but then I was a desperate man and was expecting some kind of miracle. The first thing I heard was laughter, followed by Mark informing me that I would definitely have to go in a third time. It felt like they knew what my thought processes were right then, and I almost experienced a little bit of paranoia creep into my mind. I decided it was definitely time to accept my fate and just crack on with it like all my teammates were doing. Having said that, I didn't actually know the nature of the thoughts going through the minds of the rest of the team. Maybe they were struggling too or maybe they just took it all in their stride?

Eventually, I emerged from the cabin and made my way onto the deck. Darkness was well on its way by now. The conversation between my teammates and crew was now at a minimum. I no longer witnessed the constant chatter and laughter that was evident a few hours previously. The only one constant was the endless slow rocking of the boat in random directions, and my nausea began to return.

I lent on the metal railings, which had now cooled considerably as night fell. George was still monotonously stroking his way through the water, with his green lights attached to him. I had only watched him for a matter of minutes before I heard talk of giving him his ten-minute signal. His swim was nearly over. Had I really taken that long to get dry and changed into my clothes?

Then I noticed Megan standing on the deck all prepared for her next swim. This would be Megan's very first night swim, as she had not had the opportunity to have a practice one. I was both impressed that Megan did not seem that nervous for her next stint, and also a little worried how she would cope with swimming in the dark for the first time.

When I was training for my English Channel solo swim, I had every intention of doing a practice night swim, but for various reasons, it never happened. This did cause me some degree of anxiety leading up to my swim, as I knew there was a good chance that part of my swim would be in the dark. It turned out that I was very lucky to have swum my entire swim in daylight. My first night swim came a few weeks later when I was a support swimmer for my friend Chris Pountney, on his English Channel attempt. I remember jumping into the cold, dark water in the early hours of the morning and thinking how weird it felt. It was a totally different environment to the daytime sea. At first it was rather unsettling and took some time to adjust to this different sea world. However, it wasn't very long before I actually found it quite a relaxing experience and enjoyed it more than I could have imagined.

I was now hoping that Megan would also have a similar positive experience of swimming in the dark for the first time. The whole team depended on it. Despite some deep-rooted concerns, I still remember feeling very confident that Megan would pull this off and not disappoint us. After all, she had been recommended by Cathy, and we all knew how hardcore Cathy was!

> Observer's report: 'The boat is now populated by a whole team of polar explorers. There isn't a spare layer to be found, as they protect themselves from the falling air temperatures.'

Megan dived into the cold, dark water and immediately began swimming towards George, who was now heading back to the boat. Megan did not appear to be phased at all by her first-time swimming in the dark. The sight of her gliding through the sea filled me with confidence and joy.

> Observer's report 20:06: 'Megan in, George out. George says he's fine and he's warm enough.'

> Observer's report: 'Megan is getting used to swimming by the boat in the dark. It's quite disorientating and she adjusts regularly to try and stay next to the light Neil has attached to the railings. Mark (pilot) has switched on the external boat lights and has trained one on the patch of sea in the centre of the boat. Megan's S/C (stroke count per minute) is 72. By 20:25 it's completely dark. Megan looks up from time to time and adjusts her trajectory. She is storming along.'

Megan's hour seemed to pass really quickly. I had noticed this phenomenon during our previous relay. It appeared that the further into the relay you got, the shorter each swim seemed to be. I suppose it's the same when it comes to life in general. When you are a child, a year can go on forever, but as you get older, a year passes in a flash. When a child reaches their fourth birthday, the previous year has been a quarter of their entire life, and so it must feel like a very long time as it is a large proportion of their existence. Whereas a person reaching their fiftieth birthday has only experienced a fiftieth of their life during the previous year. Maybe this gives the impression that time is speeding up as we go through life and could be the same principle that applies to the way our hour swims appear to go quicker as the relay progresses towards the finish.

In no time at all, Megan was heading back to the boat and Cathy was swimming out into the dark sea with her two lights attached to her. Cathy had previous experience of night swimming during our English Channel relay, and I knew she would just knuckle down and get the job done.

> Observer's report 21:06: 'Cathy in, Megan out. There's a short delay to get Megan on safely in the swell. Cathy adjusts well and keeps her stroke long in the waves, working with the water. S/C50. Megan says she found it hard to stay parallel to the boat. Andy finds some glowsticks and the crew attach them to the rails to make this easier for the rest of the night swim.'

As predicted, there were no dramas with Cathy's swim and she steadily ploughed her way through the waves, taking us ever closer to our target and never faltering.

On the boat we were all wrapped up warm and some were even attempting to get a little sleep while propped up or laying down in various positions. Sleep was never going to be an easy thing to achieve in the circumstances, but even a short power nap would be a welcome relief from the constant rocking on the waves and might even re-energize us a little.

Sam appeared to have a moment where she was mentally not quite prepared for her third swim. We all have moments of self-doubt, and it can sometimes be very difficult to overcome. Sam just needed a few wise words of encouragement from Neil to get her mind back in the right place and then she was once again focused on the job at hand.

The ten-minute signal was given to Cathy, and Sam was already standing there ready to go and start another round of our extraordinary relay.

Round Three:

Sam dived in again and we all hoped that this third swim would be her final one, but that was really only something we could keep our fingers crossed for as this relay had so many uncertainties about it that you could not really predict anything. Sam had clearly overcome those inner demons that had troubled her earlier and was swimming confidently.

Observer's report 22:06: 'Sam in, Cathy out. Sam stops for a moment to adjust her goggles, which have filled up with water. During Sam's next hour, the wind drops a little, but then picks up again. The wind, waves and swell are now coming directly at her. Dolphins visit again but Sam doesn't notice them. She has to stop a few times to adjust her goggles. Maintaining a S/R of 60.'

Fred's report: 'Swimming like this in the dark is a totally different experience and can be very disorientating. The relentless pace continued and they were not discouraged when the distance they had covered over the ground was adversely affected by a head on tide. Morale was still high especially during Sam's third swim as dolphins turned up to investigate. There was now the realisation that the goal could be achieved, all the team were strong and determined and barring horrendous weather it was not in the bag but definitely achievable. At times the boat was rocking fairly severely as the wind had whipped up a swell which made climbing back on board more difficult.'

Despite the tiredness and the sea sickness, we were all still feeling quite positive that we could achieve this swim. All we had to do now was to mentally prepare ourselves for getting back in for yet another hour in the cold, dark Atlantic Ocean. On the plus side, we all had each other for support and encouragement, and that's one of the best things about being in a relay together. We were all suffering in various different personal ways, but what we all had in common was that sheer determination that we would succeed as a team.

Sam did an amazing swim as she always does, and Richard once again took over from her. He stormed off in his usual style like there was no stopping him. All we could hope for now was that we could all maintain what we were doing and that there would be no dramatic change in the weather conditions. Between us we were steadily chipping away the miles towards the Isles of Scilly and we all had that dogged determination that we would reach that tiny little island, which formed a part of this archipelago off the Cornish coast.

Observer's report 23:06: 'Richard in, Sam out. Richard stops a couple of minutes later, looks at the boat for a while, then continues swimming. He stops again to adjust his goggle strap. S/R70.

The skipper, Mark, confirms that the team has covered 21nm so far. He tells Sam that she took one for the team, as he adjusted their course slightly north during her leg to make their eventual landing easier.

Richard adjusts his hat and goggles another few times during this swim, as the waves hitting his head knock them askew. He is playing a stormer, ploughing through the waves.'

It was now time for me to get ready for my third swim. This wasn't an easy process by any means. I still felt like I had not properly returned to my normal body temperature and the thought of getting back in that cold water for another hour didn't seem very appealing at all. I had words with myself. I went over in my head that I had previously swum the English Channel on my own and so this should not be a problem. Then I thought about Sam having a few issues before her third swim and she had swum the English Channel twice. I realised this was not about past swims or achievements it was about what was happening right now. Relays are very different to solo swims and the two cannot really be compared.

Obviously, there was never any doubt in my mind that I would get back in the sea and do my best hour of swimming that I could. But the mental preparation was definitely a struggle for me.

Eventually, I stood on the deck in my swim trunks and felt very nervous. The ten-minute signal had already been given to Richard and so now I just had to wait as the clock ticked away for the changeover.

Andy opened the gate for me to step down onto the platform ready to begin. The whistle was blown and as I saw Richard heading back to the boat, I jumped in. This time I held my goggle strap as I entered the water, to try to avoid any further issues with water leaking in.

As my head resurfaced, I thought to myself, *here we go*. I had to swim my heart out for the next hour no matter what. I calmed my breathing down after the initial cold shock of the water temperature and tried to get back into a good rhythm.

It had been a few years since I had last swum in the dark and I remembered that it's never as bad as you would think. In many ways it was actually quite relaxing. As I glided through the crystal clear sea, the spotlight from the boat shone down in front of me. Rays of light pierced through the water and made everything look so magical.

My jellyfish friends were still milling around just below the reach of my hands, although some were a little closer and came to say hello. These magnificent creatures looked even more amazing during the night with the light shimmering on them. It made me wonder if these were the same jellyfish that were about during the day. Were they sleeping jellyfish even though they were still moving, or were they the night shift while the day workers got some rest? I had no idea if there were such things as day and night jellyfish, but I was certainly happy that they were still keeping me company during what otherwise could have been a very lonely hour swimming in the dark.

Observer's report 00:06: 'Mark in, Richard out. Richard says the rough water pulled his hat off, hence the constant adjustments. Mark is swimming very strongly, although he cannot see where the waves are coming from. Wash from under the boat hits at irregular intervals.

After Richard's swim, there are 3.8nm to go.

Mark's stroke rate is 60. He is feeling better in the water than on the boat. He's not the only member of the team to feel nauseous on the rolling boat and several have fed the fish at various intervals.'

I enjoyed this night swim much more than I anticipated I would. I think there was something about the angle of the spotlight that made it a very different experience from my previous night swims. Or maybe it was because I was now swimming in the Atlantic Ocean rather than the English Channel? Would that really make a difference? Whatever it was, the experience was amazing. Every time I breathed out in the water, there was a wonderful sight of air bubbles being blown downwards for a short distance before stopping in their tracks and deciding to head back to the surface. During their short journey, the light shone through them, making them look magnificent and vibrant as they formed random and ever-changing shapes. My arms would pass through these bubbles of light while the jellyfish watched this extravaganza from just below. The experience was mesmerizing, and I almost didn't want it to end.

As the hour continued, the novelty of the bubble spectacle began to lose its appeal and my thoughts began to focus more on finishing my stint and getting out again. I felt cold, but nowhere near as cold as I had been at this point on my previous swim. I was looking for movement on the boat which may indicate that George was getting ready to take over from me, but all I saw was a general shuffling around.

Suddenly, I saw some arm waving from somebody on the boat, and I think I could just make out that it was Megan giving me my ten-minute signal. This was my time to understand that the end of my hour swim was in sight and that I must put in every last bit of effort I had left in me to benefit the team and bring us closer to our finish point. I gritted my teeth and swam like crazy!

Then suddenly I heard an unusually loud noise. It was a deep, strange and almost haunting sound, but I was convinced I knew what it was. I had heard this sound many times before on wildlife shows on the television. I knew, without any doubt, that this was the sound of a whale. This made me feel both excited and yet a little on edge at the same time. Was there really a massive whale just beneath me? How friendly would this whale be? I decided that I was more excited than anything else and couldn't wait to tell the others of my whale encounter.

Finally, the whistle blew, and I looked up to see George standing at the back of the boat and waiting to start his swim. It was such a welcome sight. I started swimming towards the boat as George passed me in the water. I grabbed hold of the metal handrail as the boat rocked quite violently. It wasn't an easy exit and certainly not at all glamorous, but I managed to haul myself up the few wooden steps and had many hands helping me back onto the deck.

The first thing that came out of my mouth was that I had just heard a whale. There were mixed responses to this revelation and I was asked if I was absolutely sure. I was in no doubt that a whale had called or sung from the depths below me. Everyone wanted to know exactly what I had heard, so I proceeded to give my best impersonation of a whale, much to the amusement of my teammates and crew. I felt pretty daft by this point but my conviction remains to this day. There was at least one whale in that water!

The discussion continued and it seems the most likely explanation was that the sound came from the bow thruster on the boat, but who likes a rational explanation? Certainly not me.

As much as I had enjoyed so many aspects of my swim, I finally felt like I was home and safe. All I had to do now was get dry and warm again and hopefully enjoy watching my fellow teammates succeed in this challenge.

Observer's report 01:06: 'George in, Mark out. 3.1nm to go. The tide is against the team now. Mark is convinced he heard a whale towards the end of his swim. After a bit of a chat, it turns out it was actually the sound of the bow thruster. Much hilarity ensues as Mark is gently teased by his teammates.

Once I was wrapped up warm, though still shaking, I made my way to the side of the boat to watch George in the water. He was the one member of our team, and our previous team, that I always had the least time watching, as I was busy seeing to myself following my own swim. George was a strong swimmer and was always consistently reliable and I enjoyed witnessing him making good progress towards our goal.

Suddenly, there was much excitement on board as we noticed that a pod of dolphins had decided to join George and swim with him. Their dorsal fins kept breaking the surface of the dark water and then disappearing again. This spectacle was captured in the spotlight of the boat and looked totally magical. I really hoped that George was aware of the presence of his special guests.

> Observer's report: 'George is looking strong and comfortable. S/R66. He moves away from the boat a bit so his 10 minute warning is a bit late. There are dolphins swimming with him but he doesn't see them in the inky blackness.'

> Fred's report: 'The islands grew imperceptibly closer as each hour was completed. The red lights on the radio mast on St Mary's became a useful beacon for the swimmers and skipper alike.'

Before I knew it, Megan was standing on the deck next to me in her costume and looked totally ready for her third hour in the sea. This was going to be her second night swim, and for someone who had never previously done any night swimming, she looked particularly calm and relaxed. However, we have to appreciate that someone may look calm on the exterior but you cannot see what they are feeling inside. I have no doubt that Megan would speak of this moment in a very different way.

George's time was finally up, and Megan dived into the dark water as though she had been doing it all her life. The two crossed paths and then George hauled himself back onto the deck. His work was done.

Megan shot off at some speed like she always does. Maybe this was an automatic response to the cold water and the need to quickly produce some body heat. I'm sure we all start a bit quicker for this reason, but Megan just seemed that much quicker at the start than the rest of us. It wasn't long before she got into a good steady pace.

Observer's report 02:06: 'Megan in, George out. The team are surprised he didn't see the dolphins, as they were criss-crossing right in front of him. George says he couldn't see the glowsticks, but Neil's light is a good point of reference.'

Observer's report: 'Megan S/R71. The tide has been against the team for 2–3 hours now, resulting in the forward progress of the last two hours being greatly reduced. Skipper Mark is impressed that nobody has actually gone backwards, something he has experienced on previous swims. It's now beginning to slacken. There are 2.4nm to go at the start of Megan's leg.'

As I leant on the railing watching Megan making progress through the water, I was filled with hope that we were going to succeed. Every stroke that Megan made brought us that little bit closer to our finishing point. What this finishing point would actually look like, none of us knew. What I did know was that we were gradually chipping away at the miles and had made no backwards movement during the head-on tide. I was so pleased about this and it just confirmed to me what an amazing team we had.

I kept staring at the red flashing light on the radio mast on St Mary's as it had been visible for some time. There was no way of gauging how far away this light was, but I kept focusing on it to the point where it became quite hypnotic at times. I was aware that Cathy was getting ready to get back in and so Megan's hour was almost over.

In theory we knew Cathy could complete the swim within her time slot, but we also had to respect that there were other forces at work that were out of our control. As Cathy dived in, the excitement on the boat was immense. We all hoped so much that Cathy would be the one to complete our challenge, especially as she was the team captain.

Megan emerged from the sea feeling triumphant as she had put in such a strong performance. After congratulating her, the whole team focused on Cathy. I stood there on the deck watching Cathy gently glide through the water. There was no way I wanted to miss a single second of her swim. I was transfixed, as I knew I was witnessing history being made.

Observer's report 03:06: 'Cathy in, Megan out. 1.3nm to go. Megan is a little cold but the team help her to dress and she retreats to the wheelhouse, out of the night air. Cathy says she will do her best to finish it. The team would love this to happen, since she is team captain. S/C 53. Cathy stops to adjust her goggles. The team are all watching her and point out that Cathy's long hair, piled up inside her cap, make her hat assume the shape of a streamlined cycle helmet.'

I sat down on the cold, damp deck and watched Cathy through the railings. My mind started wandering in all sorts of directions. I thought about all the situations that had led up to this moment where I was sitting in the dark watching Cathy hopefully complete a world-first swim. I remembered quite clearly the very first time I worked with Cathy on the ambulance and mentioned to her that I wanted to get a team together to swim across the English Channel. Cathy immediately said she wanted to be a part of this team. She had no real concept at the time of what this may involve. She simply signed up knowing she could overcome anything that was thrown at her. I loved Cathy's attitude and fearlessness. And now, stroke by stroke, she was hopefully going to make our dreams a reality.

Sam got ready to enter the water yet again, just in case Cathy did not quite make it to land within her allotted hour. We all hoped so much that Sam wouldn't have to get in for a fourth time.

Suddenly, a bright spotlight was shone from the boat and there in front of us was the island of St Mary's. At first, I couldn't make out if it was a beach, but it soon became clear that Cathy would have to end the swim by touching a cliff face. These were never ideal finishing points and always carried a certain amount of risk to the swimmer, especially in the dark. We were all exhilarated at finally seeing the finish point, and we were all cheering Cathy on. She paused for a moment and looked back at the boat as though not quite sure what all the noise was about. We shouted at her to keep swimming towards the light. Cathy got her head down and ploughed on.

> Observer's report 03:45: 'Land is very close. Sam is getting ready, just in case she has to get in and take over, but like her teammates, she would love Cathy to make the touch and finish the swim. With 10 minutes of Cathy's swim left, she has 0.17nm to go. There is loud encouragement from the boat. Several torches are trained on the cliffs ahead of her and suddenly the team see how close they are to finishing this most challenging of swims.'

The boat came to a stop as it could not risk getting any closer to the rocks. Cathy was now so close to the cliff in front of her and she regularly put her head up to navigate her approach. We all hoped that the waves were not too bad and she could make contact with the rocks safely. Eventually, Cathy appeared to stop altogether. It was difficult to see if she was next to the cliff but then suddenly she raised her arm in the air and waved back at us. That was it, she had made contact and the swim was complete. There was much cheering and shouts of joy from us all, together with lots of congratulatory hugs. Then we noticed that Cathy was attempting to climb out of the water. This was not necessary as the swim had already officially ended by making contact with the rock. But then we witnessed her haul herself onto what must have been a tiny ledge and stand up, waving her hands in the air. Cathy was simply making a statement that the swim was well and truly complete beyond any doubt.

I was excited beyond belief. We had just witnessed my good friend Cathy complete a world-first relay swim. I simply couldn't wait for her to make her way back safely to the boat so the whole team could celebrate together. It wasn't a straightforward swim back either, as she kept heading out of the beams of torchlight and into the darkness. We had to keep shouting loudly for her to swim directly to the boat. Maybe she was a little disorientated, which would not be unusual. Eventually, Cathy was helped back on board to the relief of everyone. Finally, we could all celebrate our amazing accomplishment as a team, and it felt totally amazing.

Observer's report: 'Everybody shouts and cheers Cathy as the time gets closer to the end of her swim leg. She gives it everything and touches the cliff at 04:05:39, after 59 minutes and 29 seconds of her one-hour swim leg. The team have made it in a time of 17 hours, 59 minutes and 29 seconds. Cathy swims back to *Celtic Fox* and there are hugs and congratulations all round. The mood is buoyant and jubilant. The team are all wrapped up cosily and celebrate together, talking through their swim.'

Instructions are shouted at Cathy as she heads to the finish.

Fred's report: 'Mark brought his boat as close as safety allowed to the cliff by Little Britain Rock of St Mary's. Andy focused the searchlight on the vertical granite wall as Cathy swam away from the boat to their goal. A dot in the distance, but then she stood up and turned to face us. The boat erupted in whoops and cheers. Emotions were still running high when she climbed back on board for the final time. Clock time 04 hours 05 minutes and 39 seconds on Thursday 16th September 2021. Swim time 17 hours 59 minutes and 29 seconds. The impossible takes time.'

The moment that Cathy reaches the finish.

This swim had taken so much organization and preparation and had not been an easy ride by any stretch of the imagination. However, this awesome swim team had gone out there and conquered this almighty challenge. We had somehow become the very first team to swim from mainland Britain to the Isles of Scilly under English Channel swimming rules.

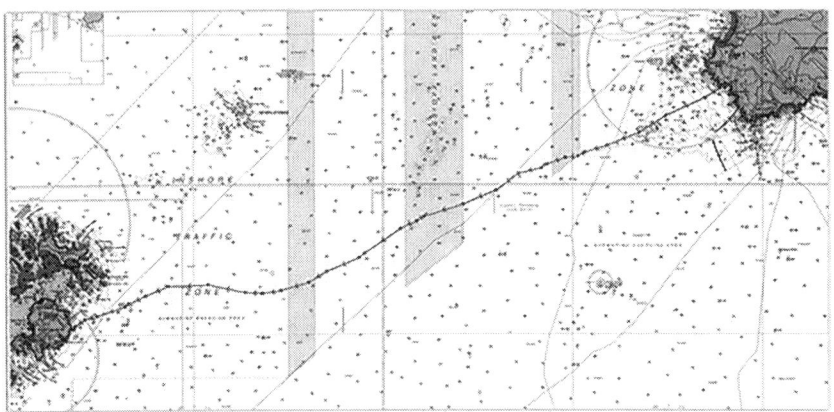

Our route to the Isles of Scilly.
17:59:29

TWELVE

VICTORY

As much as we wanted to continue celebrating our massive achievement, we were just too exhausted, and it was extremely late in the night. We also had a long boat journey back to the mainland ahead of us. Unlike our English Channel relay celebrations that four of this team was a part of, this would not be a celebratory time on the way back to England. This was sleep time, and we all tried to find a place on the boat that felt the most comfortable for us to try to get some rest. At first I sat on the deck with a few of the others, but it wasn't long before we all lay down, wrapped up in as many layers as we could find to try and keep warm on our long journey back to the mainland. My head was resting on my damp towel, which I had folded and placed on top of one of my bags. It was the best pillow I could muster up in the circumstances.

As I lay on the metal deck, I was desperate for sleep, but my mind was simply buzzing with thoughts of everything that had happened over the previous day. It was almost too much to take in and process. I closed my eyes in the hope that this would lead to some rest. Suddenly, some ice-cold salty water spurted in my face. It was a very cold awakening, not that I was actually asleep. I looked up to see that right next to my head was a hole in the side of

Trying to get some sleep.

the boat. I assumed this was a hole to allow water to flow out of the boat in times of need. However, right then it was simply a means of squirting me in the face with cold water at various intervals. These intervals were unpredictable and there could be several minutes of grace before I experienced another face full of water.

I looked around at the others. Sam was curled up on the bench; Richard had found a comfortable place at the back of the boat. I had to weigh up the odds of possibly finding a better place to try to sleep or just stick with what I had. I was fairly comfortable lying next to the others on the deck and so I decided to stay. After a while I actually got used to the cold squirts of water and even managed to chuckle to myself each time it happened.

Perhaps being tormented by the sea whilst I tried to sleep was some kind of stark reminder of the ridiculousness of this 'sport' of ours! A sport where you train so hard for something that may never even happen due to the weather or conditions. Then, if and when you get the go-ahead, you will face putting yourself through extreme hardships. The chances are you will become hypothermic and seasick during the event. That's not to mention the extreme tiredness and maybe disorientation and confusion. You will need to eat to keep your energy levels up but simply cannot face putting anything in your mouth. There are not many sports that will put you through all this and, even then, not guarantee you will even reach the finish line. In some ways I felt like I needed to be experiencing this 'telling-off' from the sea for encouraging my teammates to put themselves through all of this torture. However, I was certain that our achievement would outweigh their suffering and that I would be forgiven.

Eventually I slept, but I assume the cold water continued to soak my face. I had simply got used to it and it didn't bother me anymore. I suppose this situation is synonymous with the cold-water training that we all undertake to complete these types of swims. You just have to get used to the uncomfortable feeling of the cold against your body, or in this case my face. After a certain amount of exposure to it, you're simply not bothered by it anymore.

After a while, I became aware that others were moving about on the boat and talking. As I opened my eyes, I realized the sun had made another appearance and it was now daytime. I had obviously managed to somehow get some decent rest.

Feeling stiff and groggy, I forced myself to get up. As I stood there holding onto the railing to steady myself as the boat rocked about, I was greeted with the most amazing view of a magnificent sunrise illuminating the sky with a mixture of orange, yellow, and red and everything in-between. The reflections of light on the deep blue water were mesmerising. To the left we had the stunning south Cornish coastline and up ahead I spotted St Michael's Mount, and it simply looked magical. The whole view was almost too much to take in. It looked like the start of a perfect day.

Conversations between us were fairly quiet and subdued considering what we had just achieved. We were all just simply exhausted. I'm sure we had so much more we wanted to say, but right then it was just too much effort.

Eventually, Penzance came into view and excitement started to build as we knew we were finally going to be able to step onto dry land again. We all desperately needed this boat journey to end and to be able to stand completely still without being rocked or thrown about. What's more, we had a small welcoming party that we were all looking forward to seeing.

As the boat entered the harbour, we saw some familiar faces standing on the quayside. April, Mark and Owen were there with Cathy's parents Liz and Ian. What would they say to us? What would we say to them? Did anything really need saying? What we had just achieved said everything really, but words would still be exchanged, together with many hugs of congratulations.

We had group photos taken, although I knew I must have looked

Six Scilly Swimmers celebrate their success.

dreadful in the pictures. Stepping off the boat was an amazing experience. We were finally back on the mainland where this whole adventure had first begun the previous day. Solid ground and no movement. It felt like heaven!

I don't actually remember my journey back to our house and, if I'm honest, I can't even remember who was driving or which

With our official observers, Kate and Neil.

With our crew and observers.

vehicle I was in. My only focus was getting a quick shower and then to bed for some proper rest. I was simply mentally and physically exhausted, and right then the need for sleep was overwhelming.

Once in my amazingly comfy bed, I had a chuckle to myself regarding the enormity of what we had just endured to achieve our goal. Richard and George appeared to be asleep already, so there would be no chatter this time. That was fine by me as all I wanted to do was sleep, as there would be plenty of time later in the day to revel in our glory. I closed my eyes and I was gone.

It didn't seem long before I awoke to hear George and Richard talking to each other. The three of us made our way downstairs, and as we did so, we encountered the smell of grilled bacon. A fry-up was being prepared in the kitchen, which was a wonderful surprise. We helped carry things out into the garden where we were going to have a celebratory brunch. Of course, it was the veggie option for me.

Outside the back door were some wooden steps that led down to the garden where the table sat on the lawn. The late-morning sun was out and the day was warming up nicely. Once seated with the feast before us, a bottle of Prosecco was handed to Cathy to pop the cork. April went up the steps so she could capture the moment on her phone. As the cork shot out of the bottle and high into the air, we all cheered. Then we witnessed the cork descending and, without any hesitation, April held out her hand and somehow caught it before it hit the ground. It was almost like it had been rehearsed, and she just continued to film the moment as we all laughed at her miracle catch.

The atmosphere was simply buzzing as we stuffed our faces, sipped Prosecco and spoke about our triumphant relay swim. I could still hardly believe we had achieved a world-first swim and I'm sure the others were thinking the same. It was just a shame that Sam was unable to join us for this celebration.

The rest of the day was very chilled and, for Richard, George and me, it involved having a beer at the Lido and just relaxing. Later in the afternoon, George also had an interview on Radio Suffolk about the swim, which went very well.

When we finally got into bed that night, we were still exhausted. This challenge had certainly taken a lot out of us. I lay there in the dark talking to Richard and George about our relay. Then an idea struck me. Surely, if we were the first to do this relay swim, then we must hold the record as the fastest. I immediately began searching on my phone for the Guinness World Records official website. I had a look at various pages and found a section on setting new records. There were very strict criteria that had to be met before a new record was accepted. I read through the requirements and could not see why our swim could not be classified as such. I mentioned it to the boys, and they seemed very keen on the idea of pursuing this matter further.

The following day we went to a food and drink festival on St Ives beach, which sadly Sam couldn't make, but we had, however, planned to meet her the next day for a swim around St Michael's Mount.

Five Scilly swimmers having fun at St Ives beach.

That evening as we all sat around the table to eat, I told the others about my discovery that we may be able to claim a new world record. There was much excitement that this may be a possibility. I promised to look into it further once I was back home.

I was up quite early the following morning as I had planned to go to Land's End parkrun with Megan. I knew that Megan dabbled in a bit of running and had previously done some parkruns, so it seemed logical at the time to suggest this idea to her. Megan had obviously agreed straight away and we both took our running gear down to Cornwall with us. The one factor I hadn't taken into account was that I may have an injury from my Brighton Marathon a few days previously. My knee was still painful and I was still walking with a limp. However, I was determined not to let this injury stop me from taking part in this parkrun, as it was maybe a once-in-a-lifetime opportunity.

Megan drove us to Land's End, and as we pulled up in the car park, I was actually feeling so excited to be taking part in this event. My knee was hurting, but it was so much better than it was a few days previously. Megan and I started the run together and then she was off. Obviously, I expected this as my knee was painful and giving me issues from the outset. I simply had to limp my way around the 5km course, but that was fine by me. My only aim was to complete Land's End parkrun.

As I hobbled my way around the course, the area was simply stunning. We were high up on the clifftops with a magnificent view over the early morning sea. It was the same stretch of water that I had once witnessed two basking sharks swimming so gracefully together, having earlier swum very close to one of them and appreciated its sheer magnificence. Then, as I painfully struggled my way around the course, I looked further out to sea and recalled our experience out there in the deep Atlantic Ocean just a couple of days previously, and it just seemed like a dream now. This run was not a comfortable one by any stretch of the imagination, but to me it was a necessary one.

The final part of the course was a three-lap route near the finish point. Megan obviously finished well before me, but then she decided to join me for my last short lap. My knee was very painful by now, but I managed to keep running slowly. I was so glad to have Megan by my side to give me encouragement on this final part of the run. As I passed the finish line, I felt like I had achieved something amazing. Six days previously, I had run Brighton Marathon. In fact, I had run many marathons and many parkruns, but for some reason this parkrun felt really special to me.

Megan and I after completing Land's End parkrun.

Once back at the house, I had a quick shower and then it was time to head off to Marazion to meet up with Sam and finally get the whole team together again for probably the last time. The plan was to have a group swim around St Michael's Mount. This would be the first time the whole team had actually swum in the water at the same time, and we thought of it as a kind of lap of honour following our successful Scilly swim. It was made all the more special because our official observer Kate would also be joining us in the water.

This was a very laid-back swim. We all swam fairly close to each other and there were plenty of stops to have a chat and appreciate the wonderful view. As we approached the far side of the mount, I remembered Sam telling me that a few months previously she and a friend had decided to do this swim, but when they arrived around the back of the mount, the sea conditions became far worse, and they were forced to turn back. On this day the sea was quite calm and so I was sure we wouldn't encounter such conditions. However, as we started to swim around the back of St Michael's Mount, the wave height really picked up and we found ourselves on a bit of a water roller coaster. We were being raised many feet upwards before being plunged right back down again. At one point I went down rather fast and came to a sudden halt as I landed on a very flat but rough, barnacle-encrusted rock. It was painful and it worried me that there were rocks that close to the surface. I warned the others to keep away and we gave the island a wider berth.

Eventually, we swam our way down the other side of the mount and, despite a rather difficult exit from the sea due to the many rocks and seaweed, we finally made our way up the beach feeling triumphant once again. For me it felt wonderful that the whole team had done this swim together, and it gave me a feeling of closure. It was a time where we could all share our swimming experience at the same time and yet have no pressure on us at all. It was the perfect cool-down.

Once dry and changed, we all sat on a wall facing the sea and ate chips. There was much banter over our Scilly swim, and whilst we laughed and joked together, I couldn't help feeling rather sad deep down as I realised we would probably never all be with each other again in one place, despite the challenges we had been through as a team, in order to succeed. We had some group photos taken, then it was soon time to bid farewell to Sam and Kate, and there were many hugs and maybe the odd tear.

Six Scilly Swimmers following their lap of honour around St Michael's Mount.

That evening back at the house, the rest of us had our final meal together and a few drinks. We then had a very relaxed evening playing games and listening to music. When I say relaxed, I mean apart from the jigsaw!

On my first evening in the house, I obviously had a little curious look around, and in the front room, there was a grand piano. I was not surprised by this as I knew the house had one. However, what I discovered on the top of this piano was a very partially started jigsaw. Not even the edges had been completed. My mum was a huge lover of jigsaws, and I would often help her with them when I went to see her. So naturally I had a look and managed to put a few pieces in.

I later discovered that it was actually Megan who had brought this jigsaw for us to try to complete during the week. The evening after I arrived in Penzance I decided to try and complete a bit more of the jigsaw. Megan came into the room and immediately told me off for looking at the picture on the box. I honestly thought that was the way that jigsaws were done, by studying the picture and deciding where pieces belonged. However, according to Megan, this was cheating. Apparently, you should never look at the picture and should try to work it out for yourself. This was a very hard pill for me to swallow. Everything I thought I knew about jigsaws throughout my life had just been completely blown out of the water. Megan clearly did hardcore jigsaws!

That evening, we still had rather a lot of the jigsaw to complete, so Megan, Cathy, April and I all stood around the puzzle desperately trying to finish it before the end of the night, but it looked unlikely, especially as we were not allowed to look at the picture. Despite what we had already achieved that week, it somehow felt like we had not properly succeeded if we did not finish that jigsaw. We frantically tried finding the right pieces, sometimes passing them to one another if we thought it was on their part of the puzzle. About every fifteen minutes we would all rotate our positions so we could work on a fresh section. It was great teamwork, but then I expected nothing less.

In the early hours, Cathy and April decided to call it a night and went to bed. All the others had gone to sleep a while earlier. Megan and I decided to carry on just a little bit longer. We were both exhausted and in desperate need of sleep, but we were determined to finish that damn jigsaw. I remember having some kind of sleepy and delirious conversation about whether we should just give up and go to bed, but somehow, we came to the conclusion that we should see this through to the end. At 03:30am Megan had the honour of putting the final piece in the puzzle. It felt like such a monumental moment, although I doubt anyone else would get that.

Sliding under the duvet felt like heaven. As I lay there in total exhaustion, I wondered if I had ever needed sleep so much in my entire life.

I awoke a few hours later to hear Richard and George discussing what time they thought I may have come to bed. I interjected and explained with great pride that we had managed to finish the jigsaw. If I'm honest, they didn't appear overly impressed with my revelation, but I was satisfied that we had stuck it out till the bitter end.

After breakfast it was time to say our farewells and begin our long journey back to Bury St Edmunds. It felt strange having to say goodbye to the others, never really knowing if we would all ever meet up together again. We had all spent the week bonding, and now it was time to break away from one other. There were lots of hugs and congratulatory chat. I said to Megan, "I can't believe we did it!"

Megan replied, "I know, it's amazing!"

I added, "Yes it is! It took us 'til three thirty in the morning, but we got there!"

Megan laughed when she realized I was referring to completing the jigsaw and not our world-first relay swim.

At about 09:30am, with our luggage loaded, I climbed into the back of Richard's car and we drove off down the road, leaving the others behind. As much as I felt sad, I also could not wait to get home and back to some kind of normality. Exactly a week previously, I was at the start line of the Brighton Marathon. What a week it had been!

I arrived home late afternoon and had decided I would do absolutely nothing for the rest of the day. I would sit there on the sofa and simply not move. I think I had earned it, and the only active part of my body was my brain, which was still processing everything that I had experienced over the previous week. There was a lot to process, and much of it seemed just like a dream now. Had that all really happened to me over the last seven days? I made a mental note to myself to make sure I never tried to cram so much into such a short amount of time again.

That night I once again climbed into bed, but this time it was my own bed, in my own home, and in my own town. It was only now that I could truly relax and feel at peace. My mind was still buzzing with thoughts and memories, creating all sorts of emotions within me, but my exhausted physical body fought against this craziness and soon brought it all to a halt as I fell into a deep sleep.

THIRTEEN

A NEW WORLD RECORD

A few days later I was back at work and back to reality with a vengeance. It somehow felt like I was a different person and living a different life. There I was back in my day job as a carer and the Atlantic Ocean felt like a million miles away or in a past incarnation. Danielle and a few other colleagues asked me about the swim and showed a genuine interest, but many were probably not even aware of the adventure I had been through over the previous week. They had their own lives and were not concerned with what was going on in mine. Even for those that showed an interest, it was hard to describe what had happened and the importance of what we had achieved. They were not swimmers and some probably didn't even know or care where the Isles of Scilly were.

Less than a month after our swim we received the news that Tia had given birth to a wonderful little boy called George. Congratulations! Perhaps he would grow up to be a swimmer.

I contacted Guiness World Records (GWR) and explained what our team had achieved and enquired if this could be registered as a new world record. This wasn't an easy or quick process by any

Tia with baby George. Born 8th October 2021.

British Long Distance Swimming Association

The Executive Committee
have great pleasure in awarding this certificate to

Six Scilly Swimmers

in recognition of completing a

UK to the Scilly Islands

Inaugural Relay
in a time of 17 hours, 59 minutes, 29 seconds
on the 15ᵗʰ & 16ᵗʰ September 2021

Team Members

1. SAM JONES	2. RICHARD PEARCE
3. MARK RANSOM	4. DARREN (GEORGE) MAGUIRE
5. MEGAN SANDERS	6. CATHY FREEMAN-BROWN

Team Manager
Cathy Freeman-Brown

Amanda Bell, President

Our certificate from the British Long
Distance Swimming Association.

means, but I was so grateful that we had used the British Long Distance Swimming Association (BLDSA) to officially ratify our swim with two observers. Without this official seal of approval from a respected and recognized swimming authority, I doubt if we could have claimed this record. We had to wait several months to obtain our official certificate from the BLDSA. Once this was received, I could then proceed with our application for a new world record.

The following April we were in a position to finally announce the total amount that we had raised for the RNLI. We were overwhelmed by the generosity of the people that had sponsored us and were very pleased with our grand total. As already agreed, any money that was raised in cash would go directly to the Dover lifeboat station. We decided that it would be nice to personally hand the money over to their crew and so Richard and I travelled down to Dover, where we met up with Sam, who had arranged a meeting with them. Sam was also joined by her partner Rich and mother Sharon.

Sam handing the cheque over to the Dover lifeboat crew.

After we handed the money over and had pictures taken, we decided we simply had to get in the sea for a quick dip. It was lovely to see Sam after so many months and especially great to be back in the sea with her again. We only had a short swim as it was more of a token gesture than anything else. Then it was off to Cullins Yard for some lunch and a drink.

Eventually, it was time to say farewell to Sam and the others, and Richard and I headed off to the Premier Inn where we had booked a room, as we had decided we should make a night of it. Obviously, we couldn't visit Dover without having a drink in the famous White Horse pub and it was lovely to have a catch-up with landlord Stu Fox. Then it was on to Les Fleurs to check out the pub that had taken over the duty of allowing its walls to be signed by English Channel swimmers, now that the walls of The White Horse were completely full. It seemed strange to me that this tradition was now taking place in a different pub, and a little sad as well. But I suppose you have to move with the times and sometimes change is necessary. I was just so glad that my name was still on the wall in the oldest pub in Dover, The White Horse.

The following morning, after a walk along the seafront followed by a hearty breakfast, we made our way back home. On the journey back to Bury St Edmunds, I received a message from Vince Classen, the Honorary General Secretary of the BLDSA, saying he had been trying to get hold of Cathy, but she had not replied to his messages. Cathy is not the most efficient person when it comes to replying to, or even reading, messages, so this was no surprise to me. I called Cathy to inform her that the BLDSA had been trying to get in contact with her and we had a good chat.

The reason they were trying to make contact was to let us know that we had been awarded the 'Captain Webb Centenary Relay Trophy' for the completion of our world-first swim. This was such unexpected and amazing news for us all. Trophies were normally presented at the BLDSA annual dinner but, unfortunately, because of covid, the dinner had not gone ahead. We therefore had to arrange a time and place to be presented with our trophy, and the obvious way to do this was at one of the many swimming events that the BLDSA were organising around the country. We agreed to meet up with the BLDSA President Amanda Bell at the Champion of Champions event in Dover in June, to be presented with our trophy.

Getting team members together for such occasions is never easy and so it was just Cathy and I that travelled down to Dover for the presentation, and we were also accompanied by April. It was great to be back on Dover beach on this hot sunny day in mid-June and also lovely to get to meet Amanda Bell, who presented our trophy to us. We had a long chat with Amanda about swimming, and one thing that will always stick in my mind was when she said to us, "Others may come along and beat your record, but you will always be the first, and nobody can ever take that away from you."

Just after the presentation, I suddenly noticed Neil Brinkworth among the swimmers on the beach. He appeared to notice my presence at the same time and he walked towards me. We greeted each other with a hug. It was an absolute delight to unexpectedly bump into Neil, who was taking part in the event, and he was pleased to see that Cathy was also with me. As we all chatted, I asked Neil if he had any big swims planned. He told us that, after witnessing our swim to the Isles of Scilly, he felt that he simply had to get

Cathy and I receiving our trophy from BLDSA President Amanda Bell.

his own team together and attempt the same swim. I was absolutely delighted to hear this news and wished him the very best of luck. I was excited that another team would be taking on this challenge so soon and really hoped it would help to start a trend and make this crossing a popular one for other relay teams.

A surprise meeting with Neil Brinkworth.

Neil kindly let us use his tent on the beach as a base and, before long, we were wishing him good luck as he prepared to start the second of his three races that day. As Neil headed to the start line, Cathy and I got into our swimwear for a little dip ourselves. It felt amazing to be back in the sea at Dover and we headed over to the pier and back, with April accompanying us on her paddleboard. I still found it a bit weird that the new pier was so much closer than the old one that I had been used to swimming to during my solo training back in 2008.

Eventually, we said our goodbyes and left the beach for the warmth and comfort of Cullins Yard, where we enjoyed a lovely meal together. Then it was time once again to say farewell to Dover and head home. However, this time it felt a bit different. Dover had been such a large part of my open-water swim training experience, but now I wondered when, if ever, I would return. Would there be any other swims in the future? Maybe this was it and I would never have a reason to visit Dover again. I tried not to think too much about it as it made me feel sad.

It wasn't until October 2022 that we finally received our Guinness World Records certificate. Although it had taken over a year, the wait was well worth it. This was something that we had not set out to achieve as I only thought about it after we had completed our swim, but it was certainly the icing on the cake.

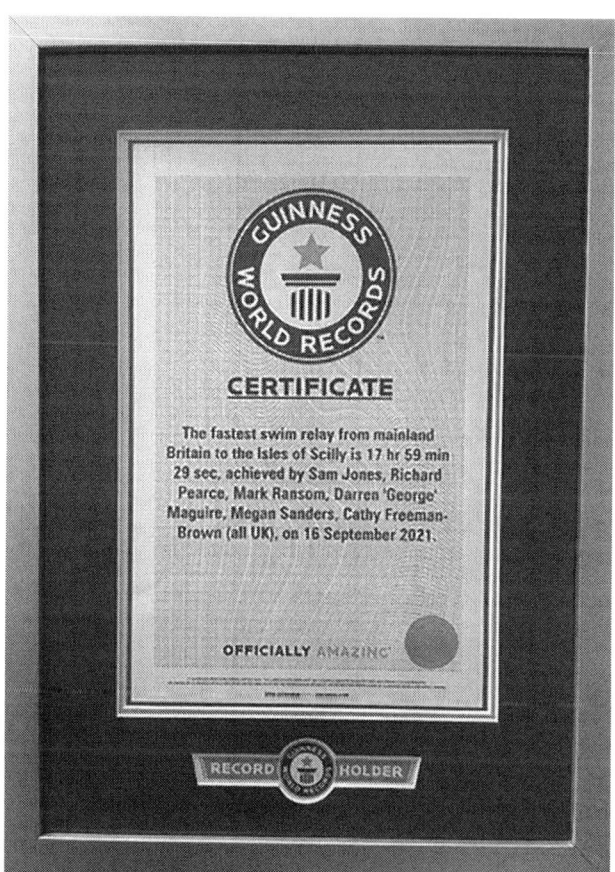

Our long-awaited Guinness World Records certificate.

Six months earlier, I walked downstairs one morning to see cards and presents waiting for me as it was my birthday. I ripped the wrapping paper off a present from Cherie to find a book written by a man called Alec Richardson who had swum across the Bristol Channel. I turned it over to read the back cover and was aware that Cherie was watching me. Then she said, "That's just to read purely for enjoyment. You know, it doesn't mean you have to launch into planning another big swim!"

I don't believe I gave an answer as I placed the book back down. It was too late...

FOURTEEN

REFLECTIONS

Writing this book was very different from writing my first book about my solo English Channel swim and subsequent relay. That book was written in two parts and both were penned after the events had taken place, and so the result of the swims were already known and the entire story had been lived and experienced. However, I actually started writing this book a few months prior to our attempt to swim to the Isles of Scilly. I knew it was a risk and maybe wishful thinking that we would be successful. I often thought that maybe I could be wasting my time as we may not make it to the Scilly Isles or even get to start the swim. Would I still have wanted to continue to write and publish a book of an unsuccessful event? Is that something others would even want to read?

I once had some feedback from my first book, and it was a criticism that I had not written about failure. Whilst I welcome all feedback on my books, whether positive or negative, I have to disagree a little with this comment, as I had written about Team East Suffolk not making it to France and the disappointment that was felt by us all. When it comes to personal failure regarding swimming, however, I must admit that I am not very experienced in this. Maybe I have just been very lucky, but I don't think that a lack of failure means I should not be writing about my successes.

One of the things I have learnt that is essential in this open-water swimming world, is the need to be flexible and adaptable, both in and out of the water. Make plans but be prepared to scrap them for an alternative. This could be anything from the start date of a big swim, as is well documented in my first book, to changing the entire swim itself, as was the case on this occasion. When it comes to planning a relay, you may need to be flexible with the members of the team too, and you may not end up with the team you had hoped for. I have to say that, for me, I have again been very lucky here as both of my relay teams were perfect on each occasion.

When we set out for another swimming challenge, we originally decided upon a swim across the North Channel. This would obviously have been a huge feat to accomplish. Then Sam said she didn't want to swim the North Channel and we had a rethink. What we came up with was a swim that no relay team had ever done before. If Sam had not opposed the idea of a North Channel relay, then we would probably never have achieved this world-first swim. Even when we were actually swimming to the Isles of Scilly, we still had not even considered that this was a potential new world record. Getting a certificate from the BLDSA to acknowledge it was an inaugural swim, and then our Guinness World Record accolade, was simply amazing. Of course, when it comes to completing a first-time swim, its true significance will only be realised if others attempt to replicate it. What we hope for is that many others will have a go at this swim and succeed. After all, you can only be true trailblazers if others follow.

Although I say being flexible in this sport is the key to success, there is, however, one thing you should never be flexible with, and that is making it to your finish point. You should always be very clear that completing your swim is an absolute certainty and there is never any negotiation on that fact. Visualise the successful finish of your swim over and over again so that by the time you are ready to start the challenge, the finish has actually already happened. I cannot emphasise this enough as an essential part of any preparation for a major swim.

This was not an easy journey for us as a team. Many of us had setbacks and some were quite major setbacks. I truly believe that one of the most important aspects of doing a team event is working together as a team. When one member of the team struggles in any way, then it is the responsibility of the whole team to support them and help them through that issue. This is the whole ethos of teamwork and probably one of the reasons why some teams succeed while others fall short.

As I was coming to the end of writing this book, I met up for a meal with an old friend. I hadn't seen Cheryl for quite some time and it was lovely to have a proper catch-up with her. If you have read my first book, you will know that Cheryl was the person I originally had a crazy discussion with (after way too many beers) about doing something really big and life-altering, like actually swimming across the English Channel.

We naturally had many other things to chat about but, inevitably, the conversation turned once again to swimming. I could hardly believe that it was almost seventeen years since we first talked about attempting that swim. If we had never had that discussion in the pub back in June 2007, then maybe I would never have swum the English Channel. That

Cheryl and I having a catch-up.

evening instigated this whole swimming adventure for me. Then I thought about our English Channel relay and appreciated the very hard work that every team member had put into achieving our goal on that occasion. If that team had never made it to France that day, then would we have been motivated to attempt yet another swim? The more I thought about it all, the more I could see the whole picture.

Cheryl was obviously the original catalyst for all my swimming exploits. Then the success of Team West Suffolk was the reason we took on this latest challenge. So, although Six Scilly Swimmers had managed to achieve a world-first relay swim to the Isles of Scilly, it probably would not have happened without the input of Tia and Ria being a major part of Team West Suffolk's success. Six Scilly Swimmers were only successful due to previous successes and all those involved in them. Everyone involved right from the very start deserves recognition of this.

We have just received the news that David Wilkie MBE has passed away aged 70 from cancer. David was one of the greatest British Olympic swimmers of all time. He was an amazing ambassador for swimming and helped so many young swimmers in their quest to succeed. I was honoured to have not only met David but also to have been coached by him in the pool many years ago. His advice and motivation were certainly a factor in my future swimming successes. He will be sadly missed. Thank you, David.

Also by Mark Ransom

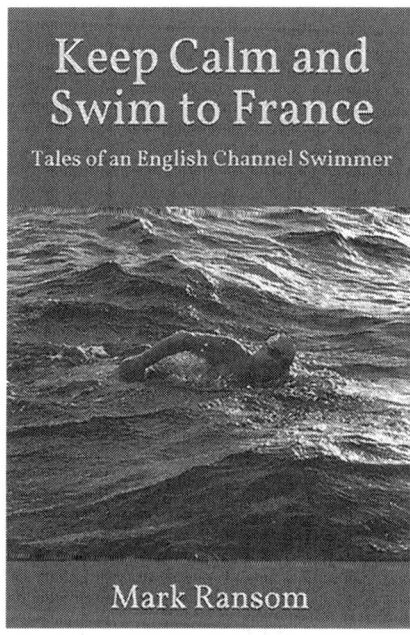

Keep Calm and
Swim to France

Tales of an English Channel Swimmer

Mark Ransom

Keep Calm and Run
100 Miles

A Story of Sheer Determination

Mark Ransom

Printed in Great Britain
by Amazon

56858440R00108